BJ BERTI

50 Fabulous
Flea Market
Makeovers

Before & After Revamped
Home Projects Using
Vintage Finds

HOME
style
BOOKS

Published by Homestyle Books/Direct Brands
Printed in the United States of America

Library of Congress Cataloging-in-Publication Data available on request
ISBN 978-1-61664-204-4 First Edition

Book Design by Michelle McMillian

Contents

Introduction

Even the most humble castoff, with some imagination, elbow grease and care can be transformed into something fabulous. Look around you and you will find all kinds of pieces ripe for making over. Not only is it fun, it is good for the environment and a way to decorate your home at a reasonable cost. With a small investment in time and material you can have the pleasure, as well as the satisfaction, of creating something special that uniquely expresses your vision.

Good salvageable pieces can be found in many places, like thrift stores, garage sales and flea markets. Even your local landfill or transfer station can yield a good find. Neighborhood pick-up days for large pieces are also good times to scout around the streets for items that are being thrown out. Keep your eyes open and you will be pleasantly surprised at what can turn up.

When you start, look for pieces that are solidly made but otherwise imperfect. It might be a battered dresser that shows signs of wear or a chair that needs refinishing and a new cover, or a shabby looking metal stool—all can be worth salvaging and transformed into a brilliant new piece for your home. Here are a few of my rules to keep in mind when you are sorting through the offerings at your local Salvation Army or flea market.

• If the price is reasonable and the piece has pleasing shape and design I will buy it even if I don't have a plan for it at the time. I imagine what I would do to it—and if I instantly can envision how it would look I usually go ahead and buy it. Look for pieces with classic design and simple lines.

• I keep my eyes open for well-crafted older pieces made with durable materials like tables, bookcases, dressers or chairs that are made with solid wood—they will be worth the investment of time and elbow grease. Or I look for pieces that have a unique shape or style, sometimes you will find something that is not that well-made but it has a special appeal or flair and can be turned into something useful or fun.

• I don't like to buy something that is really falling apart, but keep in mind that many pieces can be easily fixed with glue. It is important to look any potential purchase over carefully before buying.

Take some time to educate your eye by looking at the design magazines, books, websites and blogs. Be inspired by the things you love and work to develop your style by visiting museums, or designs shows to look at furniture and art. You will start to trust your instincts by letting yourself experiment with color and pattern. Have the vision to see beyond the apparent. Let chance guide you on your hunt and remember that any object can hold the promise of transformation.

Use this book as a starting point for your creatively and have fun transforming your flea market finds into special pieces for your home. **Just remember: there is no such thing as a worthless piece of junk.**

Porch and Deck

A **natural extension of your home,** a porch or deck is the perfect place to create an outdoor living space that's distinctly your own. Whether it's a wraparound expanse on the front of your house, a screened-in area on the side, or a redwood deck in the backyard, a porch or deck can be turned into an inviting outdoor space that's perfect for relaxing, entertaining, or enjoying meals with your family. You can bring as much style to an outdoor space as you can to an indoor one. Take some time to think about what furniture and accessories you'll need to make it functional and comfortable—or leave it to chance and take your inspiration from what turns up.

When you're shopping, try to see beyond the obvious. For example, a pair of paneled-glass doors was the starting point for constructing the simple, stylish cabinet here. Exploring ways to further enhance the glass doors, I came upon a spray-on finish called Looking Glass used to create a mirrored effect on plain glass. Some brief experimentation with the spray led to the effect of antique-looking glass I wanted. Now the cabinet looks as if it has been around for ages—just the result I was hoping for. In addition, having extra storage space on the porch is very useful—a place to organize the games, extra candles, and other items that accumulate makes the porch feel more like a living space.

Folding screens have become very popular and are quite easy to construct from both new and old shutters, doors, or windows. Their flat surfaces are perfect places to try out a new decorative technique or effect. Make a stencil pattern by tracing a large-scale floral motif, as I did here. Or combine a few different floral motifs to make a new design. Use your computer or a photocopier to experiment with the scale of your design—try enlarging (as I did) or reducing the pattern before making your stencil. Alternatively, you can use a purchased stencil or make photocopies and decoupage them onto the screen. A freestanding screen is a pretty and practical deck or porch accessory whether you use it to provide privacy for an outdoor shower, to create a cozy nook, or as a purely decorative accent.

Metal pieces in various states of rust pop up frequently at yard sales. You can leave them as they are (see Basic Techniques, page 240, for a way to preserve their natural state) or clean and paint them for a more polished look. The graceful half-moon-shaped table here was covered in rust when I acquired it. Getting rid of the rust was not too difficult, and the results were well worth the effort. Used by the front door, it performs multiple functions—as a perfect serving table or buffet, or to hold seasonal displays of leaves or flowers. Many smaller metal tables turn up at yard sales and flea markets, usually missing their original glass tops. You can simply replace the glass or take the opportunity to use the metal frame as a base for creating a new top. Used throughout the centuries from ancient to modern times, mosaic tiles are an ideal outdoor material, as they are both hard wearing and long lasting. Colorful, stylish, and easy to work with, they look good in any outdoor setting. As mosaic tiles are available in a wide range of colors, a tabletop can be made to enhance any decorating scheme. Suitable for beginners, a simple project like this one is an easy introduction to this enduring craft and results in a perfect addition to any porch.

Last, keep your eyes open for the larger attention-getting pieces of outdoor furniture like the hanging swing on page 18. Surely the pièce de résistance of any porch, a swing or its cousin, a glider, can be hard to find, but they are well worth tracking down. Wooden pieces like this swing are easily fixed up with paint, and new cushions, to soften the hard surfaces, can be made or bought. Sure to be a favorite spot for all, a swing can be the focal point of your porch or deck—and the most popular spot for sitting or napping.

Gilded Lunette Table

Gilding is really not that costly or time-consuming to do. The modern sizes used are effective and faster drying alternatives to the traditional materials. Imitation metal leaf—like the aluminum leaf used here—is a less expensive alternative to silver leaf. It looks quite nice, especially with the base coat of blue paint to complement and highlight the silvery tones of the leaf. Originally, this table probably had a marble top, but an inexpensive and easily obtainable top can be cut from frosted glass.

1 Use steelwool or a power drill with wire brush attachment to grind as much of the loose rust and corrosion off the table's surface as you can. Use a wire brush to clean the corners and crevices that are hard to reach with the drill. [photo a]

2 If necessary, apply a product like Rust-oleum Rust Reformer, following directions on the container. Then prime the table with a rust-preventive metal primer, following the instructions on the container. [photo b]

3 Sand the surface of the table lightly with fine-grade sandpaper or sanding sponge. Paint it with two coats of Cayman Blue paint. Let the paint dry completely between each coat and after the final coat.

4 Make a pattern for the tabletop: Place a large piece of paper or oaktag on the work surface. (Two or three sheets of drawing paper can be taped together if necessary.) Place the table top side down on the paper. Outline the tabletop with a sharp pencil. Have a piece of frosted glass cut to that shape [at a local glass shop].

5 Gild the table's decorative embellishments, following the directions in the gilding kit. Pay special attention to applying the size. The layer of size should be flowed onto the area to be gilded very evenly and smoothly. It needs to be as even and as thin as possible so that all areas to be gilded will be ready at the same time. Apply only one coat and do not overbrush.

6 When the size has reached tack, apply the aluminum leaf, following the instructions in the gilding kit. Use a small pad of folded cheesecloth to press the leaf onto the surface. The pad will prevent the oils on your skin from discoloring the leaf and any fingerprints from being left on the surface. Make sure the cheesecloth does not touch the size. [photo c]

7 Apply a thin coat of outdoor acrylic varnish to seal the gilded surfaces.

MATERIALS

- Metal table
- Fine-grade steel wool
- Power drill with wire brush attachment
- Wire brush
- Rust-oleum Rust Reformer and applicator
- Metal primer
- Fine-grade sandpaper or sanding sponge
- Benjamin Moore house paint in Cayman Blue #2060-50
- Household paintbrush
- Large sheet of paper or oaktag
- Pencil
- ½-inch-thick frosted glass, cut to fit
- Basic gilding kit: gilding size, book of aluminum leaf, natural-hair brush, cheesecloth
- Outdoor acrylic varnish

c

Painted Porch Swing

The perfect perch for a lazy summer day, a slatted-wood swing brings style and comfort to your porch. Changing the color from a bland, boring white to a lively green with blue accents, colors that look good in almost any outdoor setting, gives the swing a fresh, airy feel. A checked pillow adds to the retro look and softens the hard edges. When the project is completed, it is time to kick off your shoes and relax with a good book!

1 Sand the surface of the swing until smooth. If necessary, any uneven spots or cracks still remaining can be filled with wood putty.

2 Prime the entire swing with the primer. Sand lightly again. When the primer is dry, paint the flat slatted sections with two coats of Harrisburg green paint. Let the paint dry completely between each coat and after the final coat. [photo a]

3 Paint the rolled back and bottom edges and the armrests with two coats of Freesia paint. Let each coat of paint dry completely. [photo b]

4 Screw in heavy-duty eye screws on the lower front and upper back of the outside of each armrest if they are missing. There should be holes to indicate where the eye screws are meant to go.

MATERIALS

- Porch swing
- Power sander or sand-paper
- Putty knife
- Wood putty
- Benjamin Moore Fresh Start Primer
- Benjamin Moore Moorglo house paint in Harrisburg green #HC-132and Freesia #1432
- 4 heavy-duty eye screws
- 4 30-inch lengths of heavy-duty steel chain
- 6 heavy-duty quick-link connectors
- Tape measure
- Pencil
- Power drill
- 2 heavy-duty eye screws with attached hooks
- 2 34-inch lengths of heavy-duty steel chain
- 2 heavy-duty S hooks

5 Attach one of the lengths of heavy-duty steel chain to the front eye screw on each armrest using a quick-link connector and feed the chain up through the hole in the top of each armrest. [photo c]

6 Attach a second length of chain to each back eye screw using a quick-link connector. Hold the two chains on one side of the swing out so they meet and attach the chains at that point with a quick-link connector. Do the same on the other side. [photo d]

7 Hang the swing: Measure the distance between the two chains on each armrest. Measure and make a mark for each heavy-duty eye screw with attached hook on your porch ceiling, making sure to insert the hooks directly into a beam. With the power drill, make small starter holes, then screw the heavy-duty hooks into the ceiling beam. Insert the end loop of each 34-inch chain into each hook, add S hooks and hook the chain attached to the swing to the S hooks.

Mirrored-Glass Cabinet

Every porch can use some storage space. Here, vintage doors
provided the starting point, and a local car-
penter helped design and construct the cabinet. You can also pick up some new doors
at the local home center. The Looking Glass
decorative mirror-like paint used on alternating panes creates the illusion of aged
glass, adding an interesting dimension to
the cabinet front. The trick is to *not* clean
the glass first: then when you spray the finish on, the unclean surface helps to create the mottled and clouded look of old
glass.

1 Remove all hardware and hinges from doors. Fill any holes with wood putty and sand if necessary.

2 Measure your doors and adjust all the dimensions given in the material list, if necessary, to fit the length and width of the doors you are using. Cut the wood using a circular saw to the sizes given in the materials list. Prime and paint all moldings, knobs, legs, outside of sides, back, top, bottom and doors with Caribbean Teal. Paint shelves, inside of sides, back, top and doors with San Clemente Rose. (Alternatively, you could prime the pieces first, build the cabinet, and then finish painting it.)

3 Lay the two 63-inch cabinet sides flat, butted together, on the floor or a workbench. Mark "bottom" near one end of each board. Decide on shelf spacing: the shelves here are spaced to line up with the muntins of the doors. With a tape measure and pencil, make a mark on one board at each point where you want a shelf. For each point draw a line across both boards using the square and yardstick.

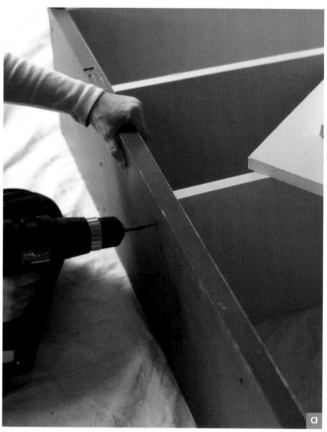

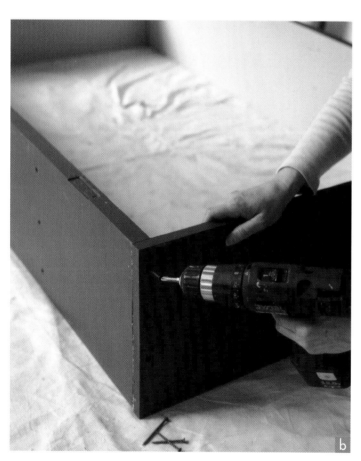

4 Mark the placement for the shelf screws: Measure and mark the center point along each line for a center screw, then measure and mark 1½-inches in from each end for two outside screws. With a drill and countersink bit, first drill a hole ⅛-inch deep on all marks, then switch to a drill bit and finish drilling all the marked holes for each shelf. The countersink holes will go on the outside of the cabinet frame. For ease in assembling later, on the insides of each board, make a chisel mark ⅜ inch below the row of holes—make a small mark at either end—to help line up the shelves.

5 From the 2 x 4 birch plywood, measure, mark, and cut a 13 x 36½-inch piece for the bottom of the cabinet frame. Place the bottom piece on top of one of the shelves flush with the back edge and centered on the shelf from side to side. Screw the two pieces together from the underside with three 1¼-inch screws. (The larger piece is the bottom of the cabinet and the smaller piece sits on top and is the bottom shelf.)

6 Mark the placement for the screws on the bottom and top pieces: Draw a line along all the outside short edges ¾-inch in from the edge. Measure and mark four holes starting 1½-inches in from the long edges, as you did for the shelves (step 3) on each short side of the top and bottom pieces. Predrill all the marked holes on the top and bottom pieces.

7 Position the metal plates for the legs on the underside of the bottom piece. Predrill holes for the mounting screws for the plates. Using a screwdriver bit, attach the plates to the underside of the bottom piece.

8 Assemble the outside of the cabinet as follows: Stand the cabinet sides up on end and fit the bottom piece in place with the smaller shelf piece on the inside and the bottom overlapping the sides. Fasten the bottom to the sides with 2½-inch screws in the predrilled holes. Set the top piece on top of the sides and fasten it to the sides with 2½-inch screws in the predrilled holes. Screw the legs into the metal plates on the bottom. [photo a]

9 Line up one shelf at a time with the chisel marks and fasten them to the sides with 2½-inch screws in the predrilled holes. [photo b]

10 Stand the piece on the legs and use a square and level to check that it is square. If it's not, bang on one corner to square up the frame. Lay the cabinet frame on the face of the lauan plywood, keeping the frame flush with the edges of the plywood. Draw a pencil line around the other two edges. With a circular saw, cut along those lines to make the cabinet back. Turn the cabinet frame onto its front and attach the back with 1-inch brads along the outside edges and along the shelves.

MATERIALS

- Two multipaned glass doors (these are 62 inches long and 36½-inches wide)
- Two 63-inch ¾ x 12 pine boards for the cabinet sides (cut 1 inch longer than doors)
- Five 34-inch 1 x 12 pine boards for the shelves (cut equal to the width of the doors minus twice the thickness of one side) of the cabinet
- One 36½-inch 1 x 12 pine board for the top (cut to equal the full width of the doors)
- One 36½-inch ¾ x 1½ pine strip for the top edge (cut to equal the width of the top piece)
- One 2 x 4-foot sheet of birch plywood ¾-inch thick for the cabinet bottom (cut to the same length as the top and the same width as the top, plus the thickness of the doors)
- One 4 x 6-foot sheet of lauan plywood ¼-inch thick for the cabinet back (cut to cover all the outside edges)
- 8-foot bed molding for the top edge
- 8-foot bullnose (or half-round) molding 1½-inches wide for the bottom edge
- Four metal plates for attaching the legs
- Four screw-in wooden legs 3½-inches high
- Four 3-inch butt hinges
- Two screw-in wooden knobs 1¼-inches wide
- Forty-eight 2½-inch #8 wood screws
- Ten 1½-inch #8 wood screws
- 1 box of 1-inch brads
- 1 box of 2½-inch finish nails
- Tape measure
- Pencil
- Square and yardstick
- Circular saw
- Miter box and saw
- Power drill with screwdriver, ⅜-inch countersink bit, 3/16-inch drill bit
- Small wood chisel
- Level
- Hammer
- Craft knife
- Paper
- Painter's tape
- Benjamin Moore Fresh Start Primer
- Benjamin Moore eggshell-finish house paint in Caribbean Teal 2123-20 and San Clemente Rose AC-10
- Paint rollers, disposable liners, and tray
- Household paintbrushes
- Krylon Looking Glass Decorative Miror-Like Paint

11 Lay the butt hinges on the inside of the doors 5 inches down from the top and 10 inches up from bottom. Mark the outline of each hinge by using a craft knife to score around all three sides of the hinge plate. This will keep the wood from splitting as you chisel out a mortise for the hinge plate to rest in. With the scored outline as your guide, chisel out just enough wood so the hinge can rest flush with the surface.

12 Predrill the holes for the mounting screws for the hinges. Install the hinges on the inside of each door. Hold the door on each cabinet frame, allowing a ³⁄₁₆-inch gap on the bottom for clearance (use shims or coins as spacers). Mark the outline of the hinges on the frame with a craft knife as in step 11. Remove the door and chisel mortises as in step 11. Hold the door in position again and predrill the holes for the mounting screws. Install the other side of the hinges on the cabinet frame. Do same with second door. [photo c]

13 With 2 ½-inch finish nails and a hammer, attach the 36½ x 1½-inch strip above the doors to the outside front of the top. The piece should be flush with the top and side edges.

14 Measure across the top front of the cabinet for the bed molding, cut a piece to size using a miter box, mitering both ends. Measure and cut the side pieces to size, mitering the corners where the side molding meets the front molding and cutting the other ends straight. Attach molding to the top edge of the cabinet with 1-inch brads. Measure and cut the bullnose (or half-round) molding for the lower edge the same way as above. Attach it to the bottom edge of the cabinet with 2½-inch finish nails. [photo d]

15 Mark the placement of the wooden knobs for the doors and predrill holes. Insert screws and thread the knobs onto the screws.

16 Apply the Krylon Looking Glass paint to the glass panes: Cover alternating glass panes with paper cut to size. Tape around all the edges with painter's tape to hold the paper in place, covering all the wood surfaces. Also cover the outside wood frame with tape. Spray the unmasked glass panes with Looking Glass spray paint, following the directions on the container. [photo e]

Tip

If you want the look of antique glass, do not clean the glass first. [photo e]

Metal-and-Mosaic Table

A good introduction to working with mosaics, this small table with its colorful top is easily made and does not require a large investment in materials. The contrast between the hard-edged tiles and the fluid, grace-ful shape of the table's S curves and leaves contributes to its considerable charm. It is quite portable—easily transported to any part of your porch or garden that requires an extra sur-face. The lively colors and small scale add up to an accent piece that is both practical and attractive.

MATERIALS

- Small metal table
- Sponge and bucket
- Household cleaner (like Soilex)
- Toothbrush
- Fine-grade steel wool
- Household paintbrush
- Benjamin Moore's Fresh Start primer (optional)
- Benjamin Moore's Moorglo house paint in Blue Lagoon #2054-40
- Tape measure
- ½-inch marine plywood cut to fit opening in tabletop
- Exterior white glue
- Container for glue
- Glass mosaic tiles in 4 shades of blue and green
- Metallic mosaic tiles in assorted pale blue-green shades
- Palette knife
- Tile nippers
- Rubber gloves
- Prepackaged grout in terra-cotta

1 Wash the metal table frame with a soft sponge and lots of water with a cleaning agent like Soilex. Use an old toothbrush to clean in the corners and crevices that are hard to reach with the sponge. Rinse well and let it dry.

2 Prepare the frame for painting by roughing up the surface lightly with fine-grade steel wool. If necessary, prime the frame with the primer. (Here the existing surface was already painted a light color, so I did not need to prime.) When the frame is dry, paint it with two coats of Blue Lagoon paint. Let it dry completely between each coat and after the final coat. [photo a]

3 Using a tape measure, measure the opening on the top of the frame and have a piece of marine plywood cut to size. Dilute the exterior white glue with a small amount of water until it is spreadable and paint the plywood on top and all four edges with the glue-water mixture. Set it aside to dry.

4 Plan the mosaic design by laying out the pieces of tile on the plywood until you are pleased with the pattern. Here I started with a border of three rows, constructed as follows: The outside row is a two-and-one alternating pattern of glass tiles in the darkest shades of blue. The next row alternates glass and metallic tiles both in similar shades of pale blue-green that are much lighter than the outside row. [photo b]

5 The third row repeats the lighter blue from the first row but alternates those tiles with a slightly different hue of medium blue. The overall effect of the three rows is that each row looks like a solid color, but the variations in tone and texture make for more interest. [photo c]

6 The inside of the mosaic is an allover staggered two by two pattern in the two lighter shades of blue green. It is symmetrical, and some of the metallic tiles are used again in the very center. [photo d]

7 Glue the tiles into place using the exterior glue. Pour some glue into a small container and, using the palette knife, butter the back of each tile and stick it onto the surface. Let it dry.

8 Using the tile nippers, cut some tiles in half to make pieces for the outside edges as follows: Hold the tile firmly between your thumb and forefinger and apply pressure to the tile at the same time as you are pressing down on the nippers. This will help the tiles to snap cleanly in half. [photos e]

9 Glue these half tiles in place, as in step 7 above, on all edges leaving bottom half of edge clear so top will fit in frame. Let it dry overnight. [photos f]

e

f

10 Wearing rubber gloves, apply the premixed grout following the directions on the package. Press the grout into the crevices between the tiles using your fingertips. Clean off the excess grout as recommended by the package directions. Let the grout dry overnight, then fit the mosaic top into the metal table frame. [photo g]

Stenciled Folding Screen

Screens can play as useful a role in your outdoor living spaces as they do inside the home. They can help make an open, exposed space feel more private and contained. Old shutters like these, or newly purchased ones from the home stores, can easily be turned into a folding screen. The surface of the screen lends itself to traditional craft techniques like stenciling, or decoupage, providing you with the opportunity to create an attractive one-of-a-kind decorative element. You can play with both pattern and scale, as this screen does, or color, to add a whimsical flourish to your outdoor decorating.

4 To stencil: Hold the stencil in place on one of the panels with repositionable spray adhesive and have the Rich Cream paint in a flat container nearby. Dip the stencil brush into the paint, but be careful not to overload it. Keep a paper towel nearby and tap the brush on the towel if you need to get rid of excess paint.

Gently dab the paint into the stencil with a pouncing motion. Try for allover distribution of paint across the surface but do not worry if it is not entirely even. Because my design runs over and onto the raised edges of the shutters, I had to hold the stencil down and push the paint into the corners. If you miss anything, you can fill it in afterward. [photos b and c]

1 Sand the surface of the shutters until smooth. If necessary, any uneven spots or cracks still remaining can be filled with wood putty. Sand again after the putty dries.

2 Prime the shutters with the primer. When the shutters are dry sand them lightly again and paint them with two coats of Bird's Egg paint. Let the paint dry completely between each coat and after the final coat.

3 To make your own stencil: Trace or photocopy the image chosen onto a sheet of Mylar, acetate, or stencil card, or make a photocopy and stick the photocopied image right on top of the card or acetate with repositionable spray adhesive. Cut out the image with a craft knife or a stencil cutter. (For this project, I worked with a photocopy of the pattern, which I traced onto a sheet of acetate using permanent marker, simplifying the design as I did so. The stencil was then cut using a stencil cutter.) [photo a]

MATERIALS

- 4 wooden shutters or panels
- Power sander or sand-paper
- Wood putty
- Putty knife
- Household paintbrush
- Benjamin Moore's Fresh Start primer
- Benjamin Moore's MoorLife house paint in Bird's Egg #2051-60 and Moor-Life house paint in Rich Cream #2153-60
- Purchased stencil

- Repositionable spray adhesive
- Flat container for paint
- Stencil brush
- Small artist's brush
- Paper towels
- 6 bifold hinges
- Screwdriver
- Furniture Glides

Optional
- Mylar, acetate, or stencil card
- Permanent marker
- Craft knife or stencil cutter

5 Allow the cream paint to dry, and add some small details, using Bird's Egg paint; to the design. [photo d]

6 Reposition the stencil on the panel and repeat the stencil instructions given in step 4. Here I staggered the pattern, stenciling the image twice on two of the panels and once on the other two panels. [photo e]

7 Small parts of the stencil can be used to add pattern to other parts of the panels if desired.

8 Hinge the panels together. You can add furniture glides to the bottom of each panel if you would like to.

Tip For Making the Stencil

Clean any mistakes when tracing the stencil patttern using alcohol and cotton swabs.

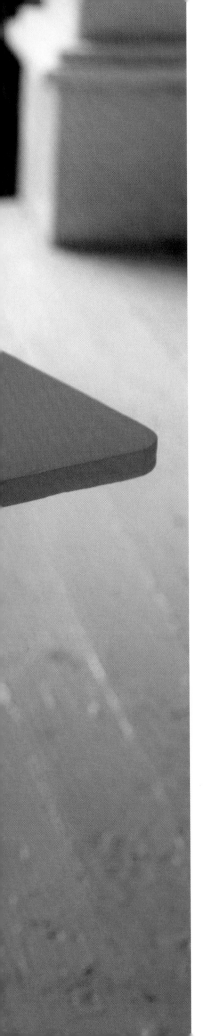

Metal Leg Table

This well-weathered low table had spent many seasons out-doors and was showing the effect of the elements: The top was peeling and the legs rusting. Cleaning and stripping the legs down to bare shining metal inspired me to use a silver-colored metallic leaf to decorate the top. If you use aluminum leaf, which is easier to find and less expensive than real silver leaf, the surface won't tarnish the way silver does and it looks just as nice. I like the simple repetition of the square shapes as they echo the square surface of the top. Outdoors on a warm day, the sun bounces and shimmers across the metal leaf.

Small patches of metal leaf can be used to brighten up other objects: A lamp shade, a picture frame, or even a small tray could be treated to some metallic flash.

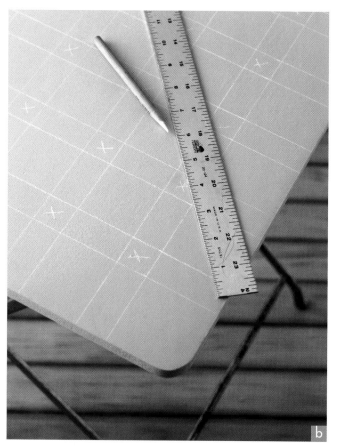

1 Strip any paint off the metal legs with paint remover following the manufacturer's directions. When the paint is completely removed, the legs can be further polished using steel wool or can be given a brushed-steel finish by using a power drill with a wire brush attachment. When you have achieved the desired result, spray legs with lacquer to protect the finish.

2 Sand the tabletop until smooth or, if necessary, peel off the top layer of plywood, then sand; any uneven spots still remaining on the top can be filled with wood putty. Sand again if necessary, then prime with the primer. Sand lightly again and paint with 2 coats of eggshell finish water-based paint. Let dry completely between each coat and after the final coat. Using a household iron, iron the wood veneer edging onto the outside rim of the tabletop. Any excess can easily be trimmed off afterward using the craft knife. Sand the veneer edging lightly, prime, and paint as above. [photo a]

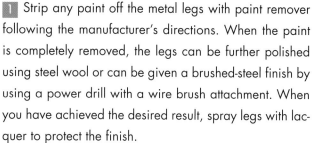

MATERIALS

- Folding table with metal legs
- Paint remover (like Zip-Strip)
- Steel wool
- Power drill with wire brush attachment
- Spray lacquer
- Power sander or sandpaper
- Wood putty
- Primer
- Eggshell finish water-based paint
- Household iron
- Iron-on wood veneer edging
- Craft knife
- Small foam roller
- White Conte pencil
- Ruler
- Painter's tape or masking tape
- Basic gilding kit: gilding size, book of aluminum leaf, natural-hair brush, cheesecloth
- Single-edge razor blade
- Matte finish varnish
- Brush for varnish
- ¼-inch-thick clear glass cut to fit tabletop

3 Using the white Conte pencil and the ruler, measure and mark 1-inch squares on the tabletop. First draw parallel vertical lines for the sides of each square starting from the center of the table and working out to each side, then draw parallel horizontal lines to complete each square. Mark the center of each of the squares to be gilded lightly with an X. [photo b]

4 Use the painter's tape or masking tape to mark off each of the squares to be gilded. If they are too close together it might be necessary to work on alternate squares and repeat. [photo c]

5 Gild the squares, following the instructions in the gilding kit. Pay special attention to applying the size. The layer of size should be flowed onto the area to be gilded very evenly and as smoothly as possible. It needs to be as even and as thin as possible so that all the areas to be gilded will be ready at the same time. Apply only one even coat and do not overbrush. [photo d]

6 When the size has reached tack, apply the aluminum leaf, following the instructions in the gilding kit. Use a small pad of folded cheesecloth to press the leaf onto the surface. The pad will prevent the oils in your skin from discoloring the leaf and any fingerprints being left on the surface. Make sure the cheesecloth does not touch the size. [photo e]

7 Before removing the painter's tape, score around the edges of each of the gilded squares with a new single-edge razor blade, cutting all the way through the metal leaf and size to the surface of the table. Make sure to cut all the way through so as not to disturb the leaf that has been applied to the squares as you remove the tape. [photo f]

8 Carefully remove the tape from the table. Apply 1 or 2 coats of the acrylic varnish to seal the surface of the gilded squares only, if desired. Place the glass on the tabletop to protect the surface.

Tips For Working With Metal Leaf

The size is ready to receive the leaf when it is almost dry but still tacky. This size became less opaque and more clear as it dried, an indication that it was reaching the right degree of tackiness. Different types of size will have different drying times and characteristics—for the best results make sure to read and follow the manufacturer's instructions carefully. Handle the leaf gently—it is very fragile. Wear thin cotton gloves or dust your fingers with talcum powder to keep the natural oils on your fingers off of the metal leaf (which becomes discolored from the contact).

Outdoor Entertaining

Once the warm weather sets in, the backyard beckons for al fresco entertaining. There are so many possibilities: a picnic on the lawn, lemonade under a leafy tree, a child's tea party for a few special friends, a sunset celebration softly illuminated by candlelit chandelier, or an afternoon visit with a few good friends. Add your personal style to any outdoor entertaining event with flea market makeovers—use your imagination to envision the perfect setting for your makeovers and don't be limited to the obvious.

One of my favorite makeovers involved a large enough dose of imagination to see beyond the obvious and a bit more ingenuity and effort: turning the seat of a down-and-out metal lawn chair into an attractive tabletop. After detaching the seat from the rest of the chair, I removed many layers of old paint and applied a fresh coat of paint to the seat. I completed my makeover by constructing a wooden base to support the top, turning it into the perfect partner for an old Adirondack chair, freshly painted to match. You could look instead for legs rescued from an old wooden table—or even for new legs from a home building store—to use as a base. Look beyond the obvious for bases to support your top—any object that can support a flat piece can become a table base. And, of course, any flat surface can serve as a tabletop.

Seating is another essential for outdoor parties. If you entertain a lot, buy any folding chair, metal or wood, that appeals to you. You can never have too many comfortable outdoor seats. The small but sweet metal settee here needed only a good scrubbing and a coat of paint to revive it. New plump cushions in a glorious yellow fabric (weather resistant, of course) add to the comfort. When you find a special piece like this, you can build an entire outdoor room around it.

Every host or hostess also needs party helpers like trays and carryalls. Whatever kind of get-together you're planning, different shapes of trays are practical additions to all your entertaining. Plain metal serving trays, which you can pick up for a song at thrift stores, can be decorated in any number of ways, including with decoupage or by spraying with glossy paint. Decorations are optional but charming. Try to pick up any pieces that look salvageable; you never know when you might need them.

Wire baskets are another useful item for outdoor entertaining. Lined with checked oilcloth, they are great for organizing cutlery, glasses, plastic food containers, bottles, napkins, and other items for picnic or an outdoor table.

Lighting creates the mood for any celebration indoors or out—extend your outdoor celebration into the evening with the imaginative use of lighting. Here a softly painted thrift store chandelier provides the illumination for a festive occasion. Turning old electric lamps and chandeliers into candelabras is an easy and fun makeover with dramatic results. Also look for interesting odd metal pieces, like gears or faucet handles, that can be used as holders for pillar candles or even mounted on a tree or wall as sconces.

Cushioned Love Seat

There are lots of these metal pieces available at reasonable prices—sometimes you can find matching sets of chairs, settees, and end tables. You can also collect them one by one as you find them. The smaller scale makes them easy to transport and quite suitable for smaller spaces like a terrace or deck. This piece was in excellent condition, only needing a surface cleaning and an easy paint job to make it look presentable. Directions are included for making the cushions, but you can also opt to have them made by a local upholstery shop or seamstress.

MATERIALS

- Metal-frame love seat
- Household cleaner (like Soilex)
- Sponge and bucket
- Toothbrush
- Fine-grade steel wool
- Disposable foam brush or household paintbrush
- Benjamin Moore Fresh Start primer
- Benjamin Moore Moorgard house paint in Buxton Blue HC-149
- Tape measure
- Yardstick
- Permanent marker
- High-density foam, 5-inches in depth
- Craft knife or electric knife
- Polyester batting
- Spray adhesive for foam
- Pencil
- Clear plastic gridded ruler
- Scissors
- Sun-resistant upholstery fabric
- Thread and 4 29-inch zippers to match fabric
- Sewing machine with zipper foot
- Pins
- Cotton cording for welting
- Household Iron

1 Wash the metal frame with a soft sponge and lots of water with a cleaning agent like Soilex. Use an old toothbrush to clean in the corners and crevices that are hard to reach with the sponge. Rinse well and let it dry outdoors in the sun. [photo a]

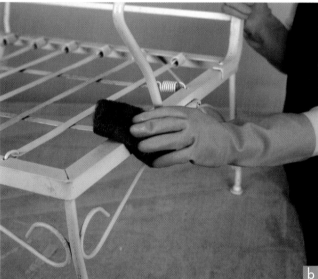

2 Prepare the frame for painting by roughing up the surface lightly with fine-grade steel wool. [photo b]

3 If necessary, prime the frame with the primer. (Here the existing surface was already painted a light color, so I did not need to prime.) When the primer is dry, paint the frame with two coats of Buxton Blue paint. Let it dry completely between each coat and after the final coat. [photo c]

4 Using a tape measure, measure the frame for the cushions. Here I wanted four cushions—two for the seat and two for the back. For the seat cushions, measure the depth of the seat and across the full width of the seat and divide the last number by two. Cut two pieces of foam to that size.

When measuring for the back cushions, allow for the depth of the seat cushions when calculating the height. The width is the same as that of the seat cushions. Cut two pieces of foam to that size.

5 Cut the foam for the cushions as follows: With a yardstick and permanent marker, measure and mark lines on the foam for each of the four cushions. If you have an electric knife, use it to cut the foam. Hold the knife parallel to the outside edge and cut straight down, like slicing through a loaf of bread, following the outline of the cushion. Or you can cut the foam using a craft knife. Cut very evenly in one smooth movement halfway through the foam, then go back and cut the rest of the way though. Check the size by placing the cushions on the frame before continuing. [photo d]

6 Cover the foam cushions: Wrap the polyester batting around each foam cushion and trim it to fit, adding additional pieces of batting to cover the sides. With spray adhesive, attach the batting to each foam cushion and set aside.

7 Cut the cushion covers: Mark the measurements for the seat cushion on the fabric and mark a ½-inch seam allowance all around the outside edges, using the plastic ruler to measure and marking as you go with the pencil. Cut out four pieces to these measurements from the fabric. Do the same for the back cushions, using those measurements.

To determine the length of the boxing strips, measure around the perimeter of the cushion form. The back boxing strip should wrap around the back corners of the cushion and extend onto the sides for 3 inches. Add 1 inch for seam allowances to the back piece. Make this piece 7 inches wide. Cut the front boxing strip to wrap around the front and sides of the cushion. Add 1 inch for seam allowance. Make this piece 6 inches wide. Split the back boxing strip in half lengthwise to insert the zipper and machine stitch it into place. Repeat for each cushion.

8 Cut enough 1½-inch-wide bias strips to use for welting on each set of back and seat cushion covers. Lay the cotton cord in the center of the wrong side of the bias strip

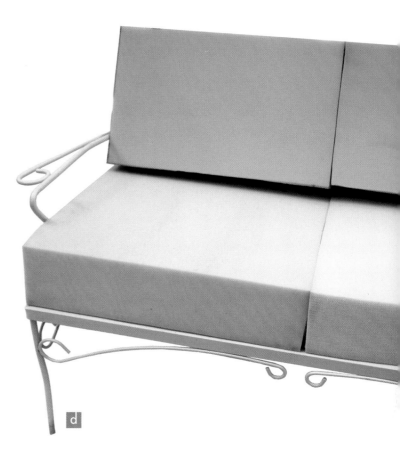

d

and fold the strip in half, encasing the cord. Using a zipper foot, machine stitch as close to the cord as possible.

9 Assemble the cushion covers: With the right sides together and the cut edges aligned, pin the welting to the top of a cushion cover and machine baste it in place. With the right sides together, sew the assembled front boxing strip to the cushion top. Stop stitching about 2 inches before the end of the strip. With the right sides together, sew the back boxing strip to the cushion top. Stop stitching about 2 inches before the end. Seam together the front and back boxing strips. Fold the seams toward the front and finish attaching the boxing to the cover. Open the zipper 3 inches. With the right sides together and the cut edges aligned, pin the welting to the bottom cushion cover and machine baste it into place. With the right sides together, sew the bottom cushion cover to the boxing. Open the zipper and turn the cover right side out. Press if needed. Repeat for the other three covers. Insert the padded cushions into each cover.

Wire Picnic Baskets

Vintage metal accessories like wire baskets, storage crates, small baskets, and buckets have a surprisingly contemporary flair because of their industrial materials. They also provide many creative possibilities for organizing and storage both inside and outside of the house. The wire baskets here can be used to transport all the necessities outside for a back-yard picnic or they can easily go into the car for trips farther afield. The oilcloth liners are easy to clean and tie on for easy removal. The patina of the metal finish can be pro-tected with a coating of linseed oil and a clear matte spray finish.

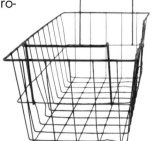

a

b

MATERIALS

- Wire baskets
- Craft knife
- Rubber gloves
- Steel wool
- Tape measure
- Pencil
- Clear plastic gridded ruler
- Drawing paper
- Masking tape
- Pins
- Scissors
- 2 yards each blue check and green check oilcloth

- White thread
- Sewing machine
- Pinking shears
- Fashion eyelets to match oilcloth
- Fashion eyelet tools
- Small hammer
- 4 yards each ¼-inch cord to match oilcloth

Optional:
- Small piece of mat board
- 1-inch-wide press-on hook-and-loop tape

1 Remove the rubber from the basket handles using a craft knife and clean the basket with steel wool if necessary. If the finish is acceptable (the green basket here was nicely weathered and still had traces of original color), it can be left as is. [photos a and b]

2 To make the liner pattern: With a tape measure, measure the basket's inside bottom length and width, then measure the depth of the basket. Draw a rectangle on paper equal to the same measurements as the bottom of the basket. Extend all the lines out to equal the same measurement as the depth of the basket and draw lines across at right angles to close the shapes. Tape sheets of paper together if necessary. You will have a pattern that is shaped roughly like a cross.

Cut the paper pattern out with the scissors and test the fit in the basket. Make any adjustments to the paper pattern needed. Make one pattern for each basket if they are different sizes.

3 Place the pattern on the oilcloth, tape or pin it into place, and cut out the shape with scissors. Repeat to make two shapes for each liner.

4 Pin two liner pieces together with the right sides facing out. Join them together by machine stitching around all the outside edges about ½-inch in from the outside edge. With pinking shears, trim the edges about ¼-inch.

5 Mark the position of the eyelets, starting about 1½-inches in from the outside corners. You will need at least two on the short sides and four on the long sides depending on your basket. Place pieces of masking tape along the top edge of the liner approximately where the eyelets will fall. Use a clear plastic ruler to measure and mark the position of the eyelets on the pieces of masking tape, moving them if necessary. Following the directions on the package of eyelet tools, use scissors to make a starter hole before removing the tape, then remove the tape and insert an eyelet into the hole. Use the eyelet tool and a small hammer to attach the eyelets to the liner. [photo c]

6 Cut the cord into 12-inch lengths and insert into each eyelet. Tie a knot on each end of the cord as close to the end as possible. Trim if necessary. Insert the liner into the basket and tie it on.

8 Make an optional divider: Make a paper pattern to fit across the middle of the basket. (The one here measures 8 inches across at the bottom and 10 inches across at the top and is 7 inches high.) Trace the pattern onto a piece of mat board and cut it out with a craft knife. Check the fit in the basket—the mat board should fit the space loosely with room to move on each side. Using the board as a pattern, place it on the oilcloth and mark around the outside edges, adding 2-inches on each side and ½-inch on the bottom and top edges. Cut out two pieces of oilcloth and sandwich the mat board between the two pieces with the right sides facing out, enclosing the board in the oilcloth. Make sure the board is centered and pin around the edges to hold it in place. Machine stitch around the shape as close to the edges of the board as possible—use a zipper foot to help you. With pinking shears, trim the edges about ¼-inch. Cut lengths of hook-and-loop tape to fit the side edges of the divider. Open a side seam and, center the loop half of tape over the seam, press into place. Mark the position on the liner for the hook side of the rope and press it in place. Repeat for the other side of the basket. [photo d]

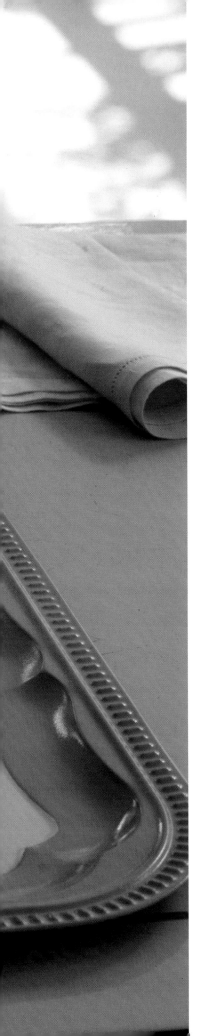

Thrift Store Metal Trays

I always see plenty of metal trays in thrift stores and at yard sales. Many have seen better days and can be a little grungy, but they clean up very well. Look for interesting shapes and sizes. The heavier metal ones, like worn-out silver plate, are the sturdiest—if you can find them at a reasonable cost. But the shape is really what you are looking for. They can be decorated in any manner from decoupage to resist spraying or simply painted in different solid colors. They can add a touch of whimsy to any space and provide practical help ferrying things back and forth from indoors to out.

MATERIALS

- Assorted metal trays
- Fine-grade steel wool
- Brown paper or drawing paper
- Pencil
- Scissors
- Spray paint in 2 contrasting colors (here ivory and pale green), 2 tonal colors (here peach and persimmon), 1 pale color (here yellow)
- Protective mask
- Repositional spray adhesive
- ¾-inch round multipurpose labels
- Painter's tape
- Craft knife
- Purchased freeze-dried leaves
- Decoupage medium
- Small artist's brush
- Small foam brush

1 All trays: Clean the surface with steel wool, wash with dish soap and water, and dry carefully. [photo a]

2 Ivory and green tray: Lay a piece of brown or drawing paper on the tray. Trace along the edges of the area you want to mask. Cut out the mask with scissors. Set it aside.

3 Spray the whole tray with two coats of ivory paint, following the directions on the can. Work outside or in a well-ventilated area and wear a protective mask. Let it dry.

4 Spray the edges of the paper mask with the repositional spray adhesive and position it on the tray, pressing the edges down firmly. [photo b]

5 Spray the unmasked edges of the tray with two coats of the pale green paint. Let it dry. Remove the paper mask carefully. [photo c]

6 Polka-dot tray: Spray the tray with two coats of the peach paint and let it dry. Position the round labels on the tray as pictured and press the edges down firmly. With the painter's tape, mask the edge of the tray. [photo d]

7 Spray the tray with two coats of the persimmon paint. Let it dry. Carefully remove the labels and painter's tape, using a craft knife to lift off the dots. [photo e]

8 Decoupage tray: Spray the tray with two coats of the pale-yellow paint. Let it dry. Position the freeze-dried leaves on the surface. Adhere the leaves to the tray by brushing the back of each one with the decoupage medium, using the small artist's brush. Press the leaves firmly and carefully into place, making sure all the edges and stems are sticking to the tray. When the adhesive is dry, coat the entire top surface of the tray, including the leaves, with the decoupage medium using the foam brush. Let it dry completely and then coat it a second time. [photo f]

Tips For Spray Painting

For even coverage when spray painting, move the can slowly across the object being painted. Continue over the outside edge of the object and then go slowly back in the other direction.

Painted Candelabra

You can easily convert an electric chandelier into an outdoor candelabra by removing the light sockets and the wiring from the piece. This is quite a bit easier and faster than rewiring it! The quick painted finish used here is an easy way to change the color while adding a nice texture and patina to the metal surface. The subtle color complements the hobnail-patterned milk glass center, and

because the technique highlights the nooks and crannies on the chandelier, it creates the illusion of an aged piece. It is also an extremely durable finish.

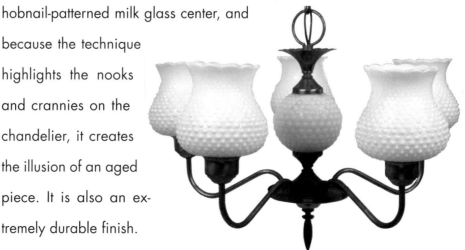

a

MATERIALS

- Metal-and-glass chan-
  delier
- Screwdriver
- Wire cutters
- Fine-grade steel wool
- Satin-finish spray
  paint in ivory
- 8 ounces Benjamin
  Moore Impervex high-
  gloss enamel in Strat-
  ton Blue HC-142

- 4 ounces acrylic
  glaze medium
- Container for mixing
  glaze coat
- Small foam brush
- Paper towels

1 Set aside the glass shades and take the chandelier apart in sections, keeping track of the sequence of parts so you can reassemble them later. If you have a digital camera, it can be helpful to take a "record" photo to refer to when reassembling the chandelier. Most of the pieces can be easily unscrewed to disassemble the chandelier. Set aside the central glass piece also.

2 When you have exposed the wiring in the center section, use wire cutters to cut all the wires running out to each arm. You should be able to then pull out the wires running up through the central post. Discard the old wiring. Loosen and remove the screws holding the electric sockets in each arm. Remove the sockets with the attached wiring and discard them.

3 Clean the metal sections of the chandelier with soap and water, if necessary, or with fine-grade steel wool. Spray them with two coats of the ivory spray paint. Let it dry for a few hours or overnight. [photo a]

4 Make the glaze coat by mixing 8 ounces of Stratton Blue paint and 4 ounces of acrylic glaze medium in a container. Add 4 ounces of water (a little at a time), stirring well.

Working on one section of the chandelier at a time, apply the glaze thickly to the surface with the foam brush and let it dry for four to five minutes. [photo b]

5 Using a wadded-up paper towel, dab at the surface to remove most of the glaze, leaving a haze of color on the surface and a buildup of color in the details. Allow it to dry. Repeat until the desired level of color is achieved. Repeat with each section. [photo c]

6 When the painted pieces are dry, reassemble the lamp, setting aside the glass shades for the arms. Save them for another use or in case you should ever want to reassemble the whole chandelier.

Tip

Use dripless candles in chandeliers or sconces. Wrap the ends of the candles with aluminum foil to make a snug fit if the holders are too large.

Metal-Topped Side Table

A very large tree branch came down in a storm, smashing this lawn chair and collapsing the metal frame on itself but leaving intact the back and seat. Taking the sections apart to see if the seat or back could be salvaged, I discovered that although the back piece was very rusty, the seat was in good shape and could be recycled as a tabletop if I had a base to set it on. An existing Adirondack chair inspired the simple carpenter shape of the legs, and a very basic frame was constructed to connect them. Now the top (formerly the chair seat) fits snugly in place on the frame, and is held in place by the lip.

MATERIALS

- Metal chair
- Vise grip
- Adjustable wrench
- Penetrating oil (like Gunk Liquid Wrench) (if necessary)
- Old newspapers or plastic drop cloth
- Paint remover for metal
- 6-in-1 painter's tool
- Protective mask
- Rubber gloves
- Stripping brush

- Soft rag
- Mineral spirits
- Household paintbrush
- Benjamin Moore Fresh Start primer
- Fine-grade sandpaper or sanding sponge
- Benjamin Moore MoorGard house paint in Marlboro Blue HC-153
- One 10-foot ¾ by 10 pine board

- Tape measure
- Pencil
- Band saw (or scroll or jigsaw)
- Oaktag or thin cardboard
- Scissors
- Power drill with screwdriver and ³⁄₁₆-inch drill bit
- Level
- Square and yardstick
- 28 2-inch #8 wood screws

a

1 Dismantle the chair by using a vise grip and an adjustable wrench to remove the bolts holding the seat to the frame. If the bolts are very rusty or hard to remove, use a product like Gunk Liquid Wrench to loosen them, following the directions on the container. Separate the seat from the frame and discard the frame or save it for another use. [photo a]

2 Spread newspaper or a plastic drop cloth over your work area. Remove the paint from the chair seat with paint remover, following the directions on the container. [photo b]

3 Scrape off the softened paint using the 6-in-1 painter's tool. Make sure to work outside or in a well-ventilated space. It might require many applications to remove all of the paint. Use a stripping brush to remove the last of the softened paint from hard-to-reach crevices. Remove any residue of the paint remover by wiping the piece with a rag dipped in mineral spirits. [photo c]

4 Paint the seat with Fresh Start primer. Let it dry. Sand the surface of the seat lightly with a fine-grade sandpaper or sanding sponge. Paint it with two coats of Marlboro Blue paint. Let it dry completely between each coat and after the final coat.

5 Measure and mark a 2-inch-wide strip down one side of the pine board. Divide the strip into two lengths measuring 13⅝-inch long and two lengths measuring 16¾-inch long. These measurements will need to be adjusted to fit the inside dimensions of your top. Cut the four 2-inch-wide strips from the board using the saw.

6 Enlarge the pattern for the table leg (or make your own). Trace the pattern on oaktag or on a piece of thin cardboard. Cut out the pattern with scissors. With pencil and pattern, trace four table legs on the remaining length of pine board. Cut the legs out by using the saw. [photo d]

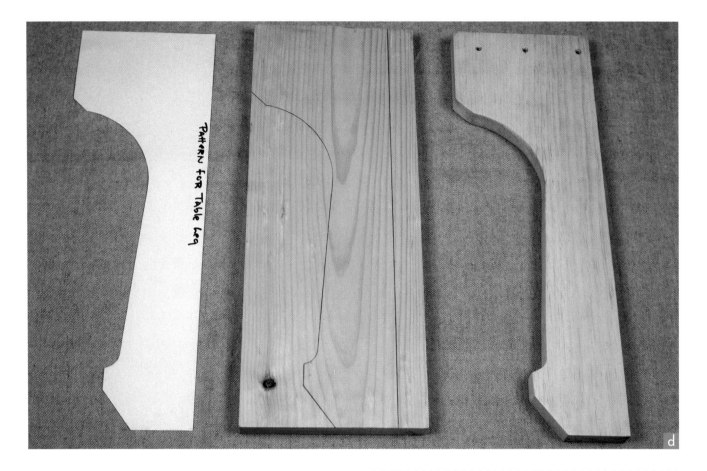

d

7 Assemble the frame as follows: Predrill two holes on each end of the shorter frame pieces about ½ inch in from the edge. On a flat work surface, stand one shorter piece on edge and butt one of the longer frame pieces against the shorter piece (use a level and square to check that the corners are square and the frame pieces level) and fasten them together with screws in the predrilled holes. Butt the other longer piece against the same shorter piece and fasten as noted above. Butt the other shorter piece against the two longer pieces and fasten as above to complete the frame.

8 Predrill three evenly spaced holes across the top edge of each leg about ¾ inch down from the top edge. Place the preassembled frame on a flat work surface and line one leg up with the outside longer edge of the frame. Fasten

Enlarge pattern for leg 570% (height should measure 20 ⅝") or adjust for desired height.

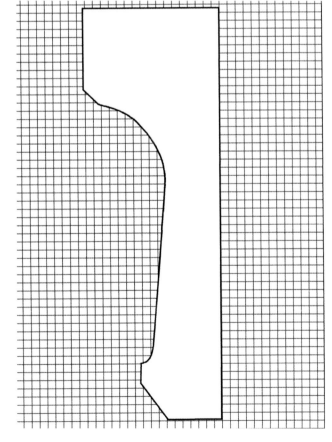

the leg to the frame with the screws in the predrilled holes. Repeat for all four legs. For additional stability, add two more screws across the top of each leg from inside the frame. [photo e]

9 Paint the frame with Fresh Start primer. Let it dry. Sand the surface of the frame lightly with fine-grade sandpaper or sanding sponge. Paint it with two coats of Marlboro Blue paint. Let it dry completely between each coat and after the final coat. Set the top in place on the frame. [photo f]

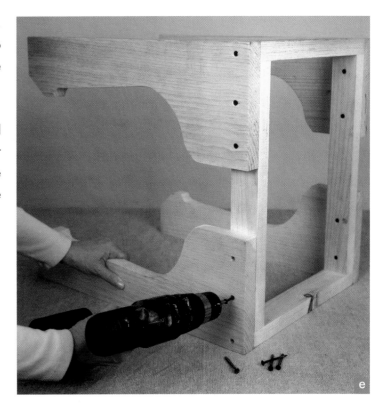

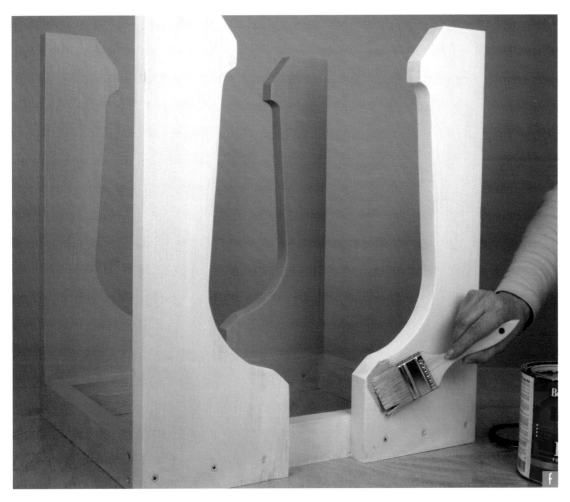

Child's Rocking Chair

A friend bought this small-scale metal rocking chair for her daughter but did not get around to fixing it up. She was delighted when I offered to fix it up —and I was pleased to have the chance to make something enjoyable for a young girl. The cottagey floral print on the cushion seemed just the right scale for this chair. Rather than go for the obvious and paint the chair pink, I chose a soft green that nicely sets off the colors in the fabric. The back of the chair looked a little bare and in need of some softening. The easy-to-make popover top fit the bill—and the ties add extra interest to the top of the chair as well.

MATERIALS

- Child's chair
- Screwdriver
- Pliers
- Permanent marker
- ½-inch-thick foam
- Craft knife
- Scissors
- Polyester batting
- Staple gun and staples
- Floral fabric
- Clear plastic ruler
- Soft lead pencil or water-soluble fabric marker
- Tape measure
- Pins
- Thread
- Sewing machine
- Household iron
- Fine-grade sandpaper or sanding sponge
- Foam brush or household paintbrush
- Benjamin Moore's FreshStart primer (if necessary)
- Benjamin Moore Moor-Gard house paint in Palisades Park #439.

1 Remove the screws holding the seat to the chair and set the screws aside until later. If the seat is not screwed in, remove it by pushing up on it from underneath.

2 With the pliers and screwdriver, remove the staples or tacks holding the seat cover in place and remove the old cover. Using the screwdriver, lift up the center of each staple and twist so one end is loose. Pull the loosened staples out with the pliers. Discard old foam or stuffing used for seat. Set the old cover aside to use as a pattern. [photo a]

3 Using the wooden seat base as a pattern, trace the cushion outline on the foam with the permanent marker. Trim the foam to fit the base using a craft knife. Cut out new padding from the polyester batting, again using the base as a pattern, allowing 3 to 4 inches extra all around for wrapping around the base. Place foam on base and wrap the batting around the foam and base and staple it in place, stretching it tightly over the wooden base as you go. Start stapling the batting to the base with a staple in the middle of two opposite sides, and then do the same on the other two opposite sides. Continue to staple on either side of the centers, spacing staples about ½-inch apart alternating op-

posite sides, pulling the batting tight. When you reach a corner, fold the batting diagonally across the corner and place one staple in the corner to hold the batting. Fold the sides in neatly and staple them into place. After you have completed stapling the batting, it can be trimmed close to the staples. [photo b]

4 Using the old cover as a pattern, cut a new one out of the floral fabric, centering the pattern if necessary, adding 4 to 5 inches extra all around. Staple the fabric in place over the batting in exactly the same fashion as above and trim the fabric when finished, if desired. [photo c]

5 Measure across the widest part of the top of the chair and as far down as desired for the popover top. Double the length and add 4 inches to that measurement. Add 3 inches to the width. Cut a piece from the floral fabric for the top using these measurements and centering the pattern if necessary. Cut four strips of fabric 2-inches wide and 20 inches long for the ties.

6 Assemble the top: Fold the ties in half the long way with the right sides together and pin down the long side, allowing a ½-inch seam allowance. Machine stitch down the long edge and across the bottom edge. Trim the seam allowance, turn the tie inside out, and press. Repeat for the others. On larger piece of fabric fold bottom edges up ½-inch and then 1½-inches to make bottom hems. Pin in place and machine stitch across both hems. Fold side edges in ½-inch and then 1 inch. Before stitching side edges, insert a tie to the depth of the bottom hem into each outer corner so they hang down below the edge. Pin in place. Pin the side edges in place and machine stitch. Stitch across the ties along the bottom edge and the top edge of the ties to hold them in place. Press using spray starch. [photo d]

7 Sand the surface of the chair lightly with fine-grade sandpaper or sanding sponge. If necessary, prime the chair with a primer. When it is dry, sand it lightly again and paint with two coats of Palisades Park paint. Let it dry completely between each coat and after the final coat. [photos e and f]

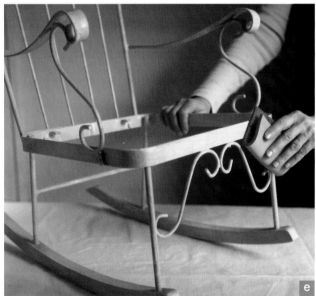

Vintage Floral Picnic Cloth

Scraps of two new printed floral fabrics are combined with pieces of a smaller-scale vintage printed chintz to make this picnic cloth. The faded patterns of the prints, both new and old, are set off by a central square, in a similar weight, of creamy off-white vintage linen. Generally, old printed cottons look best when mixed with other cottons, either new or old that are similar in tone, weight, and texture. The wide rickrack trim is a particular favorite of mine—it is used here to outline the different sections of the cloth, separating each of the fabrics and uniting the whole.

M A T E R I A L S

- About ⅔ yard each of 2 different floral fabrics
- About ⅓ yard of third floral fabric
- 19 x 21-inch piece of off-white linen or cotton
- Pencil
- Scissors
- Clear plastic gridded ruler
- Pins
- Sewing machine
- Household iron
- Thread to match fabrics
- 4½ yards 1-inch-wide off-white rickrack

1 Use a clear plastic ruler and a pencil to measure and mark four squares measuring 11¾ x 11¾ inches on the smaller piece of floral fabric. Cut the squares out using scissors and set them aside.

As above, measure and mark two rectangles each measuring 19 x 11¾ inches on one of the larger scraps of floral fabric. Cut the rectangles out and set them aside.

Measure and mark two rectangles each measuring 21 x 11¾ inches on the other larger scrap of floral fabric. Cut the rectangles out and set them aside.

Measure and mark one rectangle measuring 19 x 21 inches on the off-white fabric. Cut out the rectangle and set it aside. [photo a]

2 Lay each row out as shown, with the smaller squares in the corners and the off-white piece in the center. Working across the top row, place the side edge of each piece on top of the next piece, allowing the edges to overlap ½-inch on each side. Pin the pieces together. Sew the first two pieces together using a zigzag stitch, machine stitching down the center of the overlapped seam (see photo b). Join the third piece to the first two. Set the top row aside. Join the next two rows, as above, until all three rows are completed. Next, join the rows to one another in the same manner as above. Press the completed cloth. [photos b]

3 Finish the cloth by making a mitered hem as follows: Place the cloth right-side down on an ironing board or padded work surface. Using the clear plastic ruler as a guide, fold the cut edge of the fabric up ¾-inch. Press the fold to form a crease. Repeat until ¾-inch has been pressed up on all four sides.

Following the directions above, fold the pressed edge up an additional 2 inches. Press the new fold to form a second crease parallel to the first. Repeat until the additional 2-inch crease has been pressed up on all four sides. Unfold the second crease.

4 Keeping the fabric right-side down, use the clear plastic ruler to mark a diagonal line across each corner at the intersection of the inner crease lines. Fold each corner up toward the center along that line and press the corner into place. [photo c]

5 Fold the pressed 2-inch hem up again, repressing the crease lines, and iron each corner flat, enclosing the pressed corner fabric to form a miter. If it is too bulky, the fabric can be trimmed by cutting across the corner about ½-inch from the folded edge before folding up the hem again. Pin the hem in place and edge stitch along the folded edge. If necessary, hand stitch the mitered edges together. [photo d]

6 Measure and cut two lengths of rickrack to fit across the width and two lengths to fit down the length of the cloth. Add 1 inch to each piece for turning the ends under. Pin the rickrack in place, covering the zigzag stitching on the seams. With the sewing machine, straight stitch through the middle of the rickrack while turning the ends under to finish. Pin and stitch the two vertical lengths first, then the two horizontal strips. [photo e]

Lawn and Garden

How would you describe the perfect outdoor space? Maybe it's that quiet area of your yard you can retreat to at the end of the day, gathering your thoughts as you relax on a comfortable chair. Perhaps it's a shaded wicker chair where you can practice your newest hobby. Or, possibly, the perfect place might simply be the spot closest to your garden, where you can take in the fragrance and beauty of the flowers through the seasons from a pretty garden bench.

The possibilities for creating outdoor areas that you'll love living in are as far-reaching as your imagination. And decorating these spaces with flea market makeovers will enable you to achieve exactly the look you want. Set the stage for comfort and express your individuality; be inspired by what you see here or look for other intriguing objects to express your personality.

Serving as a focal point in even the simplest of gardens, benches come in wood, metal, and many other materials, and in styles ranging from rustic to ornate. Many classic designs in wrought iron or steel are available—even the simplest style can serve a useful function in designing an outdoor space. Look for interesting shapes like the one here, with the simple, elegant curves—even covered in rust this bench looked stylish! I added a cushion in a floral green-and-white fabric to coordinate with the soft green color of the bench.

When I first saw the wood-and-canvas lawn chair at a tag sale, complete with an attached footrest below and a canopy frame overhead, I thought how great it would be to stretch out in and unwind. It needed a new canopy cover, and I added a matching cushion for the footrest. Because the existing fabric was practically in shreds, I re-covered the entire chair. It wasn't difficult. Instead of the classic stripes, I chose a new (and weather-resistant) polka-dot fabric that, even though it is modern, has all the appeal and charm of vintage. Don't get stuck thinking that every-thing has to be vintage or flea markety; sometimes a mod-ern element is just what a piece or a room needs to make it really special. I'm convinced that the chair looks better now than when it was brand-new!

You'll always be able to find wicker pieces, in various states of disrepair, at any secondhand venue, whether it's a garage sale or an estate sale. As long as the repairs are mini-mal—a coat of paint, simple reweaving—seen-better-days wicker is a terrific buy. The two most available pieces are tables and chairs. If they are cheap enough, by all means, buy them. Easy to paint, they blend in well with almost any deco-rating style, depending on what color and fabric you choose. White has become the tra-ditional color for wicker, but black can look very fresh, especially paired with cushions or pillows in a classic mattress-ticking fabric. Bright colors are dramatic and fun, and they can work well in both traditional and modern settings. A scratched top on a wicker table can easily be camouflaged with de-coupage —or perhaps a mosaic top made from shards of thirft shop china if you are more ambitious.

Wooden folding chairs are another frequent flea mar-ket find—and a sensible purchase for any additional seating you might need. These chairs are practical and portable, but they're also plain. You can easily spruce them up with paint in a solid color or a simple, long-lasting decorative paint effect. You can also add tie-on seat cushions or simple-to-sew, easy-fitting slipcovers.

From the woolen throw fashioned from old sweaters to the wicker table decoupaged with flowers to the graceful garden bench, use the projects in this chapter to inspire you to turn your lawn and garden into an outdoor space of charm, grace, and comfort.

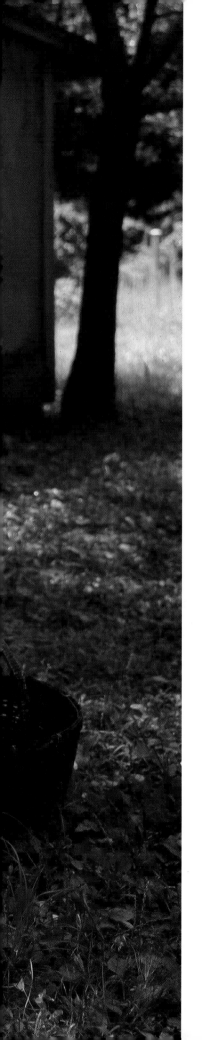

Curved Iron Bench

This lovely metal bench with a curved back had certainly seen better days when I rescued it from my friend Stuart's deck. It had been left outside for many years and was almost entirely covered in rust. A little work with a circular drill and wire brush got rid of the worst areas, then I treated it with Rust-Oleum Rust Reformer, a product that chemically converts rust into a smooth, paintable surface so there's no need to sand to bare metal. The oblong pillow in a tonal floral pattern adds an extra touch of luxury and comfort.

MATERIALS

- Metal bench
- Power drill with wire brush attachment
- Wire brush
- Rust-Oleum Rust Reformer and applicator
- Rust-preventive metal primer
- Fine-grade sandpaper or sanding sponge
- Benjamin Moore Impervex enamel paint in Stratton Blue #HC-142
- Household paintbrush

1 Use a power drill with wire brush attachment to grind as much of the loose rust and corrosion off the surface of the bench as you can. Use a wire brush to clean in the corners and crevices that are hard to reach with the drill. [photo a]

2 If necessary, apply a product like Rust-Oleum Rust Reformer, following the directions on the container. Prime the bench with a rust-preventive metal primer, following the directions on the container. [photo b]

a

b

3 Sand the surface of the bench lightly with fine-grade sandpaper or sanding sponge. Paint the bench with two coats of Stratton Blue paint. Let the paint dry completely between each coat and after the final coat.

Tip

Rust-Oleum Rust Reformer chemically converts rust into a smooth, paintable surface, so there's no need to sand to bare metal. It is compatible with most paints.

Polka-dot Lawn Chair

Well worn but still usable when I bought it, this folding chair needed new canvas for the seat and back and was totally missing the fabric canopy. Luckily, it still had its matching footrest—frequently these are missing by the time these chairs turn up at flea markets. Refinishing the frame is easy. It is a little more time consuming to make the new fabric pieces, but they are simple to construct, as they only require straight-sewn hems on the side edges. The amusing lime green polka-dot sun-resistant fabric is a change from the usual awning stripes these chairs generally sport and is the perfect color for any outdoor setting.

a

1 Carefully remove the old fabric from the chair. Label each piece using a permanent marker and set them aside; these will be your pattern pieces.

2 Sand the frame lightly with fine-grade sandpaper or sanding sponge. (If necessary, remove any finish first with paint remover.) [photo a]

MATERIALS

- Folding lawn chair
- Permanent marker
- Fine-grade sandpaper or sanding sponge
- Satin-finish tung oil
- Soft rag or cheesecloth
- Sun-resistant outdoor fabric
- Pencil
- Clear plastic gridded ruler
- Tape measure
- Scissors
- Pins

- Household Iron
- Thread to match fabric
- Sewing machine
- Ribbon trim or bias edging
- ½-inch-thick foam
- Hand sewing needle
- Staple gun and staples
- Small hammer
- Brass upholstery tacks

3 Apply tung oil with a soft rag or cheesecloth, following the directions on the container. Repeat as needed until you have achieved the desired finish. Set the frame aside and let it dry completely. [photo b]

4 Use the original three fabric pieces as patterns for the chair seat and back. Lay the old pieces out on the sun-resistant outdoor fabric, centering the pattern carefully. Add 1½-inches extra to all of the long sides for turning back and hemming. Add 3 inches extra to the top and bottom edges for wrapping and stapling the fabric pieces to the frame. If the edges will show, as they do on the upper backrest section here, add an additional inch to each end so the raw edges can be turned under and hidden before tacking. (If the original fabric is missing, just measure the length and width where the fabric seat, back, or canopy will go, adding additional for hems and wrapping as above, or seam allowances if needed.) [photo c]

5 Cut out the seat pieces along the drawn lines. Turn the long sides under ½-inch and then ½-inch again, pin, and machine stitch into place. Press the hems carefully with an iron. [photo d]

b

6 Cut the fabric for the canopy. (In this case, I had to work from measurements, as the original was missing: Measure the length and width of the frame and add 2 inches to each measurement.) Turn the fabric wrong side up and bring each corner together to form a right angle seam, pin, and machine stitch together to form the canopy. Trim the excess fabric for the corner seams and press. Cover the raw edge with ribbon trim or bias edging and stitch.

7 Cut one piece of fabric for the footrest cushion. (Again, take measurements if the original is missing: Measure the length and width of the footrest, then double the width and add 1 inch to each measurement for seam allowances.) Cut four pieces of ribbon trim 24 inches long for ties. Fold the fabric piece in half the short way, right sides facing in, pin a ½-inch seam, and machine stitch. Press the seam open and center the seam in the middle of the back. Position the ribbon ties along the inside of the top edge seam allowance, making sure the ties fall to the inside. Pin a ½ inch seam and machine stitch. Trim the fabric at the corners, turn it right side out, and press. Cut the foam to size and insert into the cover. Pin the seam closed along the lower edge. Hand sew it closed.

c

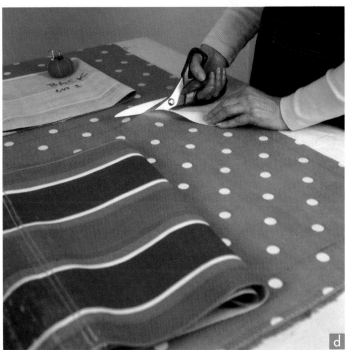

d

e

8 Wrap the fabric piece over the bottom seat frame and staple it into place. Wrap the chair back around the posts and turn the raw edges under. Hammer decorative brass upholstery tacks to hold the back in place, setting them about 1 inch apart. Staple the long piece into place, wrapping the excess around the frame, and trim if necessary. Fit the canopy top into place over the frame and tie on the footrest cushion. [photo e]

Decoupaged Wicker Table

This wicker table looks entirely different with its coat of fresh cream paint and artfully scattered country garden flowers—quite a change from its previous dingy mustard and dark green colors. The top surface is still a little uneven—the idea was not make it perfect—but fresh and pretty. I would not suggest leaving it outdoors in bad weather, but coating the whole top surface with two layers of the decoupage medium after adhering the flowers makes the table suprisingly durable. It should hold up well with many years of use. The small woven detail in the wicker base of the top is highlighted with some lavender paint.

MATERIALS

- Wicker table
- Fine-grade sandpaper or sanding sponge
- Putty knife
- Wood putty
- Household iron
- Iron-on wood-veneer edging
- Craft knife
- Household paintbrush Benjamin Moore Fresh Start primer

- Benjamin Moore Moor-Glo house paint in Rich Cream #2153-60 and Plum Perfect #1371
- Die-cut flowers
- Small square artist's paintbrush
- Decoupage medium
- Large foam brush
- Extra-fine-grade steel wool

1 Sand the tabletop until it is smooth. If necessary, any uneven spots or cracks still remaining can be filled with wood putty. Using a household iron, iron the wood-veneer edging onto the outside rim of the tabletop. Any excess can be trimmed off afterward using a craft knife. Sand the veneer edging lightly and the tabletop again, if necessary. [photo a]

2 Prime the entire table with the primer. Sand it lightly again. When it is dry, paint it with two coats of Rich Cream exterior paint. Let the paint dry completely between coats and after the final coat.

3 Punch out and arrange the die-cut flowers and leaves in a pleasing pattern on the tabletop. Brush the back of each flower and leaf with the decoupage medium using the small

a

artist's brush. Press the flowers and leaves firmly and carefully into place, making sure all the edges are sticking to the tabletop. [photo b]

4 When the adhesive is dry, coat the entire surface of the tabletop, including the die-cuts, with the decoupage medium using the foam brush. Let it dry completely and apply a second coat. When it is dry, lightly go over the top with extra-fine-grade steel wool.

5 If desired, paint the woven wicker detail on the tabletop base with Plum Perfect paint. [photo c]

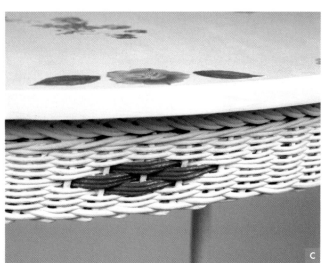

Felted Patchwork Throw

The recycling of woolen fabrics is nothing new. Old or new woolen sweaters, especially if they are boiled and felted—either by design or by accident—are suitable for cutting up into squares or other shapes and joined to make a patchwork throw or blanket. Thrift stores hold racks of sweaters in a large range of colors that are perfect for this purpose. Even raiding your or your friends' closets can turn up a suitable woolen garment past its prime. Here the luxury of the velvet and pleated-satin trims contrasts with the understated smoothness of the knitted squares, adding a touch of extravagance and playfulness to this small throw.

a

b

MATERIALS

- 4 or 5 wool sweaters
- Scissors
- Household iron
- Heavyweight mat board
- Rotary cutter
- Cutting mat
- Pencil
- Clear plastic gridded ruler
- Pins
- Thread to match background color and trim
- Sewing machine
- Purchased binding
- Optional trims

1 Turn the sweaters inside out and cut each sweater apart along the seam lines. Leave the ribbing on the lower edge of the body and sleeves intact. Starting at the lower edge of one side seam, cut up the side seam of the sweater and down the sleeve seam. Do the same on the opposite side seam. Cut as close to the seam lines as possible. Open the sweater flat, then cut around the sleeve seams to detach the sleeves from the body. Cut the neck ribbing off and then cut through the shoulder seams on each side. You will have four pieces from each sweater. Set the neck ribbing aside or discard it. With an iron, steam-press each section flat.

2 Make a template out of the heavyweight mat board— the one used here is 6 inches square. Use the template, rotary cutter, and cutting mat to cut squares from the sweater sections. Plan the squares to take advantage of any patterns the pieces might have. You can use the lower edging or ribbing if it is not too wide, otherwise it is better to cut squares from the other parts. [photo a]

3 Arrange the squares in a pleasing pattern, moving them around until you are satisfied with the color placement. This throw has 8 rows of 7 blocks. Once you have decided on your design, make stacks of the rows starting with the lower row. Stack the blocks with the first square you pick up on the top and finish with the last square on the bottom. Pin a piece of paper with the row number—1, 2, etc.—to the top square in each stack as you finish the row. [photo b]

c

4 To assemble the quilt, work on one row (one stack) at a time. Take the top square in a row and pin it to the next square with right sides facing, and machine stitch to join them. Take the next square and join it to the first two, and continue in this fashion until the whole row is joined together. Be careful to follow the stacked sequence. You will have a strip of 7 blocks stitched together. Machine stitch each square to the next one using a zigzag or overlock stitch if your sewing machine has one. Keep the paper label pinned to the first square in each row. When all the rows are completed, steam press each seam as flat as possible.

5 Pin the first row to the second row with right sides facing, matching the seams as you pin across the row. Machine stitch the rows together. Continue until you have joined all the rows together. Steam-press again along the seams, pressing as flat as possible. [photo c]

6 Apply purchased binding to the outside edge. Add additional trims if desired. [photo d]

Tip

Use a washing machine to felt old wool sweaters if you can't find any at the thrift stores. Set the machine cycle for hot wash and small load. Place the sweater in a small mesh bag and throw it in the washing machine. Add a small amount of detergent and run through the wash cycle, Then either rinse the item by hand (to prevent further felting) or run it through one gentle rinse cycle. Let it spin briefly in the washer to remove any excess water. If you rinse by hand, put the sweater back in the machine to spin briefly. Lay the sweater flat to dry.

d

Embroidered Daisy Tote

A less then perfect scrap of embroidery on unbleached cotton twill in a sunny daisy pattern was the starting point for this summery tote. The scrap is backed with linen and edged with a multitoned green rickrack whose colors complement the design and help to hide some marks on the edge of the fabric. The embroidered piece appears to be made from a preprinted panel—which were read-ily available in the first half of the twentieth century. It has the pared-down, simplified charm typical of American embroidery. Constructing the tote is really quite simple and easy.

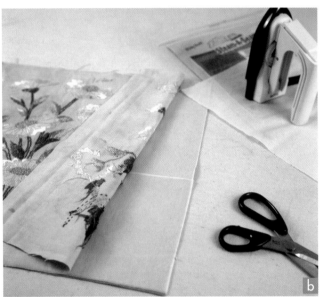

MATERIALS

- Embroidered panel
- Pencil
- Clear plastic gridded ruler
- Scissors
- 1½ yards of pale green (or other color to match panel) linen
- Pins
- Fusible web
- Household iron
- Thread to match fabric and trim
- Sewing machine
- 40 inches of 1inch-wide multigreen (or other color to match) rickrack

1 With a ruler and pencil, mark a 19 x 16-inch rectangle on the floral embroidered fabric, centering the design. Cut it out with scissors. [photo a]

2 With a ruler and pencil, mark a 19 x 16-inch rectangle on the green linen. Cut it out with scissors. Use it as a pattern to cut four more pieces the same size from the green linen. Set two pieces aside for the bag lining, two pieces for the back, and the fifth will be used as the backing for the embroidered piece.

3 Cut a piece of fusible web to size and, following the directions on the package, position the fusible between two pieces of linen with the right sides of the linen facing out. With the iron, again following the directions on the package, fuse the two pieces of linen together. This will be the back of the bag.

4 Do the same with the second piece of linen and the floral embroidered fabric to make the front of the bag. Set front and back pieces aside. [photo b]

5 Assemble the lining: With the right sides facing, pin the two lining pieces together along the side seams and along the bottom edge. Machine stitch them together, allowing a ½-inch seam allowance. Press all the seams to one side. To make the bottom shape, with the lining still inside out, flatten one corner so the side seam is centered and the corner forms a triangle. Measure an equal dis-

tance up each side of the triangle from the point and place pins across the intersecting line to form the base of the triangle—refer to photo c. Machine stitch across and press along that line, folding the corner under the bottom toward the center. Repeat on the other side. Pin the points of the triangles (or corners) into place along the bottom seam and tack them down, if desired. [photo c]

6 Assemble the outer bag: With the right sides facing, pin the front and back pieces together along the sides and along the bottom edge. Machine stitch them together, allowing a ½-inch seam allowance. Press all the seams to one side. To make the bottom shape, with bag still inside out, flatten one corner so that the side seam is centered and the corner forms a triangle. Measure an equal distance up each side of the triangle from the point and place pins across the intersecting line to form the base of the triangle—refer to photo c. Machine stitch across and press along that line, folding the corner under the bottom toward the center. Repeat on the other side. Pin the points of the triangles (or corners) into place along the bottom seam and tack them down, if desired. Turn bag right side out.

7 Assemble the handles: cut two 6 x 28-inch strips from the linen. Cut two 2½ x 26-inch strips from the fusible web, piecing the fusible if necessary. Position a strip of

fusible down one side of a linen strip and fold the strip back on itself along the edge of the fusible, leaving ½-inch of linen exposed. Following the directions on the fusible package, use the iron to fuse the piece together. Fold the extra ½-inch of linen over to cover the long raw edge and press into place. Fold the handle in half again the long way. The handle will at this point measure 1¼-inches wide. Pin it together along the edge and top stitch along each long edge to finish. Press. [photo d]

8 Assemble the bag: Turn and press ½-inch of fabric to the inside along the top edge of both the bag lining and the outer bag. Pin the handles into place on the inside of the outer bag, allowing 2-inches on each handle end to fall below the top edge and spacing each handle end 8 inches apart. Machine stitch the handles into place. Place the lining inside the bag with the raw edges facing each other and pin them together along the top edge. Machine stitch along the edge. Pin the rickrack into place along the top edge of the bag and machine stitch it into place. The finished size of the bag is 18-inches wide and 15-inches deep. [photo e]

Flower Holder and Shelf

These small metal pieces are perfect starter projects—the results are quite dramatic and easily achieved. Unlike a larger piece that has many surfaces and corners, these are easily and quickly stripped of their painted finishes, so the time and work involved are not as daunting. Frequently, larger pieces have also acquired many layers of paint. These types of small-scale metal pieces generally have a single layer, perhaps two, of paint that is easily removed. It is always something of a surprise to see what kind of surface emerges, but that is part of the fun. If you like the look of the raw metal, it will need to be protected after stripping by spraying with a clear lacquer finish – or you can finish the piece with a coat of metallic spray paint.

1 Spread newspaper or a plastic drop cloth over the work area. Remove the paint from the metal pieces with paint remover, following the directions on the container.

2 Scrub off the softened paint using the stripping brush. Make sure to work outside or in a well-ventilated space. If necessary, apply a second coat of remover. Use an old toothbrush to remove the last of the softened paint from hard-to-reach narrow crevices. Remove any residue of paint remover by wiping the piece with a rag dipped in mineral spirits. [photos a and b]

3 Once the metal is stripped, avoid letting it come in contact with water, which can cause rust to form. To protect the metal finish, spray the pieces with two coats of clear spray lacquer or a metallic spray paint. Let the lacquer or paint dry completely between each coat and after the final coat. [photos c and d]

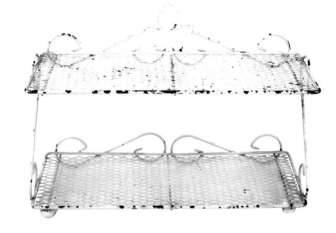

Antique Wooden Trellis

This well-weathered trellis found at a junk shop had a nicely distressed finish that was worth preserving. It's too fragile to be used in the garden, where it would be exposed to the elements, but it's perfect for a sheltered spot on the porch. Adding a mirror behind the diamond-shaped opening provides an easy trompe l'oeil effect and creates an illusion of depth. Look for elegantly shaped tall and narrow terra-cotta pots for the vinca vine—they complement the shape of the trellis and are more interesting than ordinary terra-cotta pots.

1 To determine the size and shape of the mirror, place paper over the opening on the back of the trellis and trace its outline with pencil. Use a ruler to straighten the lines. Cut out a pattern and lay it on the trellis to check. Make any corrections to the pattern, if needed. Mark the front (mirror) side of the pattern. Bring the pattern to a glass store and have them cut a mirror to size.

2 Attach the mirror to the back of the trellis using clear plastic mirror holders. If needed, make spacers out of small squares of wood lath or mat board to fit between the hangers and the mirror. [photo a]

3 Fashion hangers out of the floral wire: Bend a piece of wire around the upper middle section of a terra-cotta pot until the ends meet and cross. Leaving one end long, use needle-nose pliers to twist the shorter end around the long end to make a circle and hold it in place. [photo b]

4 Take the circle off the pot and, using the pliers, continue to twist the shorter end around itself to hold the open circle in place. [photo c]

5 Bend the other, longer end of the wire in half and back on itself. Use the pliers to twist the end around itself to hold it in place and form a loop for hanging. Slide the hanger back on the pot and push it up as far as it will go. The loop should extend slightly above the rim of the pot—if not, re-fashion the hanger or make another one. Make two more hangers and slide them onto the other two pots. [photo c]

M A T E R I A L S

- Trellis
- Paper
- Pencil
- Clear plastic gridded ruler
- Mirror cut to size of opening in trellis
- 4 clear plastic mirror hangers and screws
- Wood lath or mat board
- Screwdriver
- 3 terra-cotta pots
- Needle-nose pliers

- Broken crockery or pebbles
- Trowel
- Container-potting mix and water-storing granules
- 5-way garden tool or small knife
- 3 vinca vine plants
- 3 small flat-head nails
- Hammer
- 3 18-inch lengths of heavy-duty cloth-covered floral wire

6 Place a piece or two of broken crockery or some pebbles in the bottom of each pot over the drainage holes to prevent the soil from washing out. If you are not using potting mix that has water-storing granules mixed in, add some yourself to the mix. Fill the pots ¾ full with the potting mix.

7 Release the vines from their pots and plant them in the terra-cotta pots. If the roots are very tangled and ingrown, cut them apart with a 5-way garden tool or small knife and tease them out from the root ball before planting. Secure the plants in place by adding more potting mix. Press down firmly on the potting mix around the plants and water thoroughly.

8 Hammer three small flat-head nails into the trellis for hanging the pots, one in the center and one on each side, staggering them if desired, as shown in photo. Attach the trellis to a wall or hang it in a sheltered place. Hang the terra-cotta pots on the nails. [photo d]

Lamps and Shades

lighting is one of the most important elements in a home, and for me, it really determines how comfortable I feel. The right balance between light and shadow is a key element in any room —think about how bright overhead lights make you feel alert in an office setting and then picture yourself reading in a cozy chair in the warmly lit corner of your living room. Lighting is also one of the easiest and fastest ways to transform a space. Finding distinctive lamps or creating them from interesting architectural elements you unearth at flea markets or elsewhere requires only minimal effort. The end result is lamps that are both unique and affordable.

I found wiring a lamp very intimidating at first, but after a few attempts, I discovered how easy it really is. (If the thought of working with electrical wiring makes you nervous, just remember a lamp wire does not have electricity running through it until it's plugged into an outlet.) Follow the directions on page 117 for hot to rewire a lamp using prewired plugs.

Finding the right shade for a lamp is a little more challenging, but it's the most creative part of the process. The only real way to tell which shade best fits the lamp is by actually seeing how the shade will look on the base. Always take the lamp base with you when you go to pick out the shade, and try as many different shades as possible. You'll know instinctively when you've hit the right combination—they'll just look right together.

However, there are a few basic concepts to keep in mind when shopping for a lamp shade:

- Certain shapes work better on certain bases. Coneshaped shades complement bases that are wider at the bottom; bellshaped shades look best with vase and urn-shaped bases; oval, square, and rectangular shades are good matches for correspondingly shaped bases.

- The bottom of the lamp shade should float just above the top of the lamp base. A frequent mistake is choosing a lamp shade that is too big for the lamp; if you are torn between two, go with the smaller scale one. The harp (the metal bracket that supports the shade), if there is one, is easily removable and can be replaced if it's too tall (or short) to accommodate the shade you pick.

- If you are finding it difficult to choose, remember that in terms of materials, a simple paper shade is frequently the most appropriate choice.

Once you get a feel for pairing lamp shades and bases you might like to try to make your own shades. If a lamp's existing shade looks in balance with the base but is not the right material or color, use it as the starting point for the new shade. But if you are starting with nothing, you'll first need to figure out the best shape and proportions for the new lamp shade. Follow the guidelines above, or experiment with lamp shades around your home. Decorating magazines can also serve as a fast source for inspiration. All of these exercises should give you a good idea of the shape of the lamp shade you're looking for.

Once I decide on the shape for my new shade, I make a rough scale drawing of the base and shade on graph paper to check that the proportions work with each other. Don't be afraid to experiment a little until you are satisfied with the overall look; buy extra sets of rings (these determine the top and bottom circumference of the shade) in different sizes if you still aren't sure—they are a minimal investment for a wonderful handmade shade that will shed a lovely light for a long time.

Painted
Wood Lamp

I had this beautiful turned wood column for a long time—I think it was meant to be a candleholder as there is an opening on the top. I thought it would make a lovely lamp someday and was waiting for the right idea. Inspiration struck when I saw a similar idea for a painted lamp and shade in a decorating magazine. As the column needed a little more weight at the bottom I added an extra piece to make the base more stable and then painted both the lamp and the shade the same bright color. Using a bottle lamp kit makes this a very easy conversion—they are easy to find in the big box home stores.

MATERIALS

- Wood column candlestick
- Rubber gloves
- Paint remover (like Zip Strip)
- Paper towels
- Synthetic steel wool pad
- Wooden clock face (for base)
- Power drill
- 1½-inch wood screw/washer
- Screwdriver
- Glossy finish spray paint
- Protective mask
- Metal washer with opening to fit threaded rod
- Make-a-Lamp kit (the bottle adapter kit includes socket with push switch, cord set, rubber bottle adaptors, threaded rod and hardware)
- Harp/harp bottom
- Pliers
- Wire cutter
- Fabric lamp shade
- Lamp finial
- Pressuresensitive felt

1 Working on one small section at a time, apply paint remover to wood column following the directions on the container. Work in a well-ventilated space and wear a protective mask and rubber gloves. After 15 minutes the finish will start to soften. [photo a]

2 Wipe off as much of the old finish as you can with paper towels, then use a medium-grade synthetic steel wool pad to remove the rest. If necessary, apply a second coat of paint remover and repeat the process. [photo b]

3 Make a base for the lamp by centering the wood column on top of the wooden clock face. Mark the center point in the base and pre-drill a hole to fit your size wood screw. Before screwing them together widen the opening on the underside of the base, using a 1⅛-inch drill bit, to accommodate the washer and screw head, so the finished lamp will sit flat.

4 Spray the column, metal washer and lamp base with 2 coats of the spray paint, letting the paint dry between each coat. Work outside or in a well-ventilated area and wear a protective mask. Let dry completely, then screw the base to the column working from the underside of the base. [photo c]

5 Insert the cord set through the hole in the side of the socket and then pull out some extra wire at the top so you have plenty to work with. Split the wire and make an underwriter's knot. Strip the ends of each wire, exposing ½-inch of bare copper strands. Twist the strands of each wire tightly together, then wrap the neutral wire (covered with ridged insulation) clockwise around the silver terminal screw, tightening the screw securely over the loop. Wrap the smoother hot wire clockwise around the brass terminal and tighten. Snap the socket body in place and replace the insulating cardboard sleeve and the shell. [photo d]

6 To assemble the lamp: slip the appropriate size rubber adapter onto the threaded rod, then tighten with the included hardware, leaving some of the rod exposed at the top. Insert the adapter into the top of the wood column. Place the painted washer on the threaded rod, add the harp bottom and screw the lamp socket onto the rod, tightening the set-screw to hold it in place. [photo d]

7 To protect the inside of the lamp shade before painting cover the spokes of the top ring with paper or wrap with painter's tape. Cover the inside of shade with paper taped in place along the inside edges. Spray the shade with 2 or 3 coats of the spray paint, letting the paint dry between each coat. Work outside or in a well-ventilated area and wear a protective mask. Let dry completely. [photo e]

8 Press or glue a precut piece of pressure-sensitive felt to the bottom of the lamp. Attach the harp, place the lamp shade on top, and screw in the finial.

Glass
and Metal
Chandelier

I acquired this 1950s chandelier on a family trip to the Midwest three years ago, when some friends who had moved into a new house where it had originally hung offered it to me. Of course I had to take it. The chandelier wasn't in terrible shape, just a little dark and dingy. In a different home than ours it might have looked fine, but I wanted something lighter and prettier. I decided to try painting it blue and green and ivory in an attempt to recreate the colorful Venetian glass chandeliers I fell in love with on a trip to Italy years ago.

Anything made of metal, not just chandeliers, can be painted in a similar fashion. look for small garden tables, hanging shelves, and holders for plants decorated with natural forms like leaves or flowers.

MATERIALS

- Chandelier
- Screwdriver
- Dish soap
- Ammonia
- Old toothbrush
- Fine-grade steel wool
- Masking tape
- Ivory spray paint
- Small artist's brush
- Sign painter's lettering paint in bright green and robin's egg blue
- ¼ yard off-white linen fabric
- Sewing machine or hand sewing needle
- Cotton thread

1 Remove the decorative plastic sleeves and the inside insulating sleeves from the candle sockets at the base of each arm. Loosen the terminal screws on either side of the socket and detach the wires from the screws. Unscrew the candle sockets from the threaded rods in each arm. Lift off and set aside. Carefully inspect the wiring; if it is obviously worn or damaged, the chandelier will need to be rewired. Take the rest of the chandelier apart by unscrewing the small threaded round head pins holding the decorative glass florets in place. Set aside all of the parts. [photo a]

2 After removing the candle sockets, lift off and set aside the 2 leaf-shaped round metal pieces and the metal ring that sit at the base of each arm. [photo b]

3 Clean all the glass pieces thoroughly using water with dish soap and a little ammonia. An old toothbrush can be useful for scrubbing the dirt out of crevices. Rinse well and let dry. Clean all the metal parts of the lamp and prepare the metal surface for spray painting by rubbing down all the pieces with fine-grade steel wool.

4 Wrap all the exposed wiring with masking tape to protect it from the spray paint. Spray the metal armature of the chandelier with 2 or 3 coats of ivory spray paint, letting the paint dry between each coat. Make sure to spray the underneath areas as well. Let dry completely. [photo c]

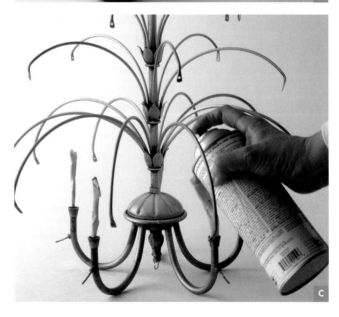

5 With the small artist's brush, paint the larger metal leaf-shaped pieces with 2 coats (letting dry between coats) of the bright green paint and the smaller metal leaf-shaped pieces and the metal rings with 2 coats of the robin's egg blue paint. [photo d]

6 Use the small artist's brush to paint the small details on the chandelier armature with 2 coats of paint and the dome-shaped centerpiece with 2 coats. Let everything dry completely. [photo e]

7 To reassemble the lamp, first put the painted leaf-shaped pieces and rings back on the arms, then replace the candle sockets. Reattach the lamp wires to the candle sockets following the directions on page 117. Lastly, reattach the glass florets to the metal brackets.

8 Cut a long rectangle out of the linen fabric, about 5 inches wide and 8 inches longer than the hanging chain. Sew a narrow hem at the top and bottom and fold in half the long way with the right sides together. Sew the edges together to make a tube that will fit over the chain. Turn right-side-out and slip over the chain before hanging the lamp.

Pressed
Glass Lamps

Lamps exactly like these are frequent finds at flea markets, house sales, and thrift shops. In fact, more than once, I've bought a single lamp and then a few weeks later come across a matching one at a sale or flea market. My favorites are those of clear glass. They're so pretty and useful that I've decided to snap up each one that I see. You can even disassemble them and recombine the parts to make new lamps. To refurbish lamps like these is a simple matter. Use the techniques below to restore the luster to any metal parts that have become rusty and pitted. Each piece should be numbered before you take the lamp totally apart so it can be easily reassembled later.

MATERIALS

- Lamps
- Masking tape
- Permanent marker
- Wire cutters
- Screwdriver
- Steel wool
- Dish soap
- Chrome or glossy finish spray paint
- Ammonia
- Old toothbrush
- Scrub pad
- White vinegar
- Cord with attached plug

1 Take the lamp apart by unscrewing the lock nut holding the threaded rod in place under the base of the lamp. When you unscrew the socket as well, the lamp will start to separate into sections. Stick a piece of masking tape onto each piece and number sequentially with the marker. If you have a pair of lamps, take them apart one at a time, leaving one intact for reference. [photo a]

2 If the cord needs replacing, cut at the bottom of the lamp. Squeeze the socket shell on the side where the word press is imprinted, and lift it off the socket base cap. Remove the insulating sleeve and loosen the terminal screws to disconnect the old wires. Pull the old cord through the lamp. Save the original socket. If it's in good condition, it can be reused. [photo b]

3 Clean any rust off the metal parts with steel wool. Wash any nonmetal parts as well as the metal parts in dish soap and water. Rinse well and let everything dry. [photo c]

4 Spray the nonglass and metal pieces with 2 or 3 coats of the chrome (or glossy) spray paint following the directions on the can, letting them dry between coats. When spray painting the pieces, stick the numbered piece of masking tape in front of each piece on the paper before you spray paint it. Let dry completely. [photo d]

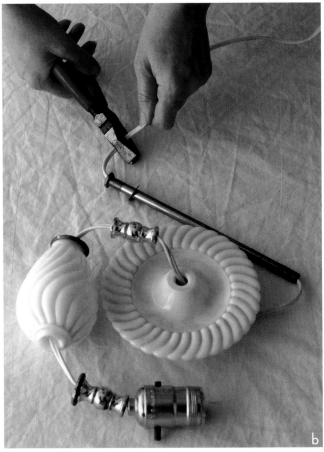

5 Clean all the glass pieces thoroughly inside and out using water with dish soap and a little ammonia added. Use the old toothbrush to scrub the dirt out of crevices. A design painted on milk glass can be removed by scrubbing with a synthetic scrubbing pad and hot soapy water. When everything is clean fill the sink with cool water. Add a small amount of white vinegar to the water and rinse the pieces carefully. Dry everything thoroughly. Reassemble the lamp and rewire the lamp and socket following the directions on pages 117. [photos e]

6 Add a purchased shade, or make your own using the instructions on pages 128-131. [photo f]

Fabric
Lamp Shade

Simple milk glass bases like these can be paired with almost any fabric that suits your color and decorating scheme. For a fresh look in a little girl's bedroom choose a small scale floral on a light background. Use a cottagey, flower print to add a cozy touch to an adult's bedroom. A ½-inch gingham check makes for an informal, country-inspired shade. Ticking (used on the shades here) is one of my all-time favorite fabrics. It has its own special appeal—depending on its setting it can add an understated charm to a more formal interior or a touch of refinement to a more casual scheme. When using patterned fabric make sure to bind the edges with a contrasting color for a more finished look.

a

MATERIALS

- Existing lamp shade (or 1 set of top and bottom lamp shade rings and a pre-drafted arc pattern to fit rings)
- Metal straightedge
- Permanent marker
- Brown kraft paper
- Scissors
- Craft knife
- Heat-resistant pressure-sensitive styrene
- Small weights
- Soft lead pencil
- 1 yard fabric for lamp shade
- Soft white eraser
- Craft glue
- Square-tipped artist's brush
- Clothespins
- Wax paper
- Clear plastic gridded ruler or compass
- Cotton twill tape, $\frac{13}{16}$-inch wide

b

1 To make your own arc pattern based on an existing shade, with the straightedge and the marker, draw a line slightly longer than the height of the shade at the lower left corner of a piece of brown kraft paper. Align the seam of the lamp shade with that line. Roll the lamp shade to the right, tracing its path at the top and bottom edges along the paper, marking the outline of the shade as you continue to roll it over the surface. When you reach the seam again, stop and make a vertical mark on the paper at the top and bottom to indicate the back seam line. Remove the shade from the paper. Connect the vertical marks and add ½-inch to the right edge of the pattern for the back seam overlap. The resulting arc pattern can be cut out, using scissors for the curves and a straightedge and craft knife for the straight ends. [photo a]

2 Lay the pattern on the styrene side of the laminating material. Place weights on the pattern to keep it from moving and trace around the outside edges with the pencil. Mark the ½-inch seam allowance as well. Cut out the arc with the scissors and craft knife as above. Erase any pencil lines except for the seam allowance.

3 Iron the fabric if needed and place it face-down on the work surface. Peel a few inches of the protective paper backing from the right-hand edge of the styrene backing and position it on the fabric, paper-side down, to line up with the straight edge (selvage) of the fabric. Reach under the arc and remove the remaining protective covering while smoothing the arc into place on the fabric. [photo b]

4 Cut the excess fabric away from the laminated arc, allowing ½-inch strip of extra fabric at the right-hand edge for folding to the inside. With the brush, apply a thin, even coat of glue along the entire length of the ½-inch strip and fold the fabric to the inside of the shade. Press in place and let dry for a few minutes. [photo c]

5 If you are using the rings from the original shade, remove the material and sand off any remaining adhesive. Place the rings on a flat surface. If they are not flat, bend gently to straighten.

6 Hold the bottom spokeless wire ring in one hand. Place the bottom center front of the arc on the wire ring and fasten the edge to the ring with a clothespin. Fit the shade into shape around the ring, fastening it as you go with the clothespins, working toward the left until you reach the outside edge. Return to the center front and fit the right half of the shade to the ring. Repeat for the top ring. Adjust the fit so the top and bottom of the shade fit evenly around the edge of the rings and there are no gaps. With the back seam facing you, lightly mark with pencil the top and bottom seam overlap. [see page 143, photo e]

7 Remove the clothespins and set the rings aside. Place the shade on a work surface with the right side up. Check that the seam allowance is straight. Turn the shade over and with the wrong side faceup apply a thin, even coat of glue along the entire length of the back seam overlap, keeping within the line of the inside edge of the seam allowance. Lifting the edge of the shade, hold it so the right side is facing you and apply a thin, even coat of glue along the entire length of the seam allowance on the outside (right side). [photo d]

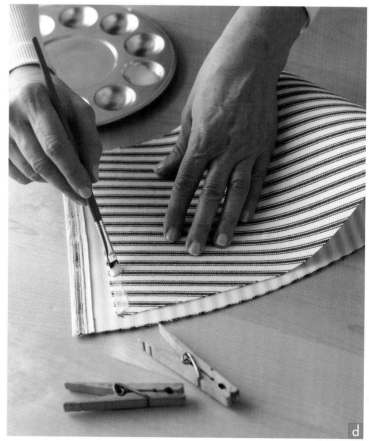

8 Bending the shade into shape, line up the top edge along the pencil mark and fasten with a clothespin. Secure the bottom edge in the same fashion. Hold the glued seam together for a few minutes until the glue sets, then place, seam-side down, on a piece of wax paper. Remove the clothespins and place small weights along the back seam. Let dry for 15 to 20 minutes, removing the weights when the glue is completely dry.

9 Stand the shade on the work surface with the top resting on the table. Apply a thin line of glue along the bottom inside edge of the shade, rotating the shade as you work. Ease the bottom ring into place starting at the center front, positioning the weld in the ring slightly to the right of the back seam. Fasten the ring in place with the clothespins, making sure the ring is positioned evenly inside the shade. Repeat with the top ring, pulling the ring up from inside the shade and positioning one of the top ring's 3 spokes in line with the back seam of the shade. Let the glue dry for 20 minutes and then remove the clothespins. [see page 144, photo g]

10 Bind the top and bottom edges of the shade to the wire rings with cotton twill tape. Draw a guideline around the top and bottom edge, using a clear plastic ruler or a compass. Cut a piece of tape to fit the top edge of the shade; square off one end of the tape. Starting at the squared end, apply glue to the lower half of the first few inches. Press the tape into place, starting ¼-inch to the left of the back seam and just covering the marked line. Allow the glue to set for 1 minute. Continue to apply the glue to the lower half of the tape, working in 9- to 10-inch segments, holding the tape away from the shade. Press the tape in place as before, making sure it is smooth and even. Continue until you reach the back seam. Using the back seam as a guide, trim the tape perpendicular to the edge of the shade. Apply glue to the full width of the tape at the back seam. Overlap the edges and press into place. [see page 144, photo h]

11 On the top ring only, use the scissors to make small slashes in the tape where the spokes connect to the wire ring. Apply a thin, even coat of glue to the inside half of the tape and press in place to the inside of the shade, rolling and molding the tape over the top of the wire. Turning the shade on its side, reach inside the shade and use your fingernail to crease the edge of the tape around the wire. Repeat for the bottom edge, omitting the slashes for the spokes.

Applying a Decorative Trim

Additional decorative trims, such as ⅜-inch velvet ribbon or biasfold trim, can be used to further embellish the lamp shade. Leave a 1-inch tail at the starting end of the trim. Apply glue to the underside of the first few inches. Press in place on the top edge of the shade, starting the glued portion ½-inch to the right of the back seam. The bottom edge of the decorative trim should just cover the binding. Continue around the shade, following gluing directions as for the tape above, until you are within 1½-inches of the back seam. Allow the unglued end of the decorative trim to lay over the starting tail. Using a small sharp scissors, cut through both layers of trim perpendicular to the edge of the shade. Glue the ends and press into place. Repeat on the bottom. [photo e]

You can use either a predrafted arc pattern from a lamp supply source or make your own arc pattern as explained below.

Here is an easy formula for making an arc pattern for a basic cone-shaped lamp shade. Start by measuring the diameters of the top and bottom rings. You'll also need to determine the height of the proposed lamp shade. With these measurements and a simple yardstick compass, you'll be able to create an arc pattern that can be used to make a custom-sized shade to fit your lamp. If you want to save the pattern, it can be drafted on a large piece of paper, cut out, and then traced onto your material (see page 128), or you can draft the pattern directly onto the styrene backing or any other lamp-shade material of your choice.

1 Draw a vertical line corresponding to the height of the lampshade (AB in the diagram).

2 Draw two lines corresponding to the diameters of the bottom ring (CD) and the top ring (EF), perpendicular to and centered on the top and bottom ends of the vertical (AB) line.

3 Draw a line connecting points D and F, extending it up about two times its length. Repeat for the other side, connecting points C and E.

4 Label as X the point where DF crosses CE.

5 Calculate the length of the bottom arc (DH) by multiplying the length of the line CD by pi (3.14) and adding ½-inch for the side seam overlap. Use the yardstick compass to draw the bottom arc (DH). Anchor the compass point on X and place the pencil on D, moving the pencil to the left to scribe a semicircle (or arc) of that length. Check the length measurement with a tape measure. This forms the bottom arc (DH) for the shade pattern.

6 Repeat for the top arc by multiplying the length of the line EF by pi (3.14) and adding ½-inch for overlap. Use this measurement for the length of the top arc (FI), which can be drawn by placing the compass point on X and the pencil on F. Use a tape measure to check the length.

7 Cut out the pattern (or actual shade) using a metal ruler and craft knife for the straight edges and scissors for the curves.

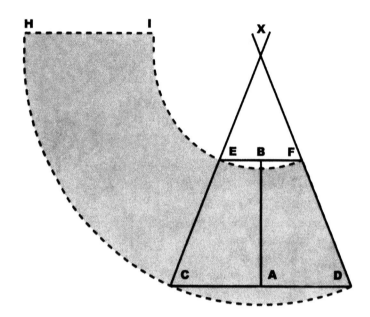

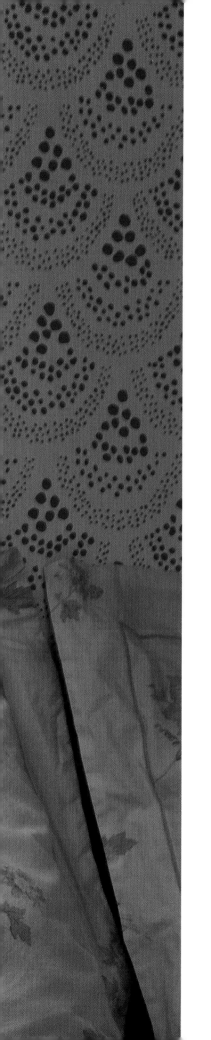

Pressed
Glass
Sconces

As with the pressed glass lamps previously (page 122) these are frequent finds and easily transformed to suit your decor and mood. Each of these sconces was treated in a similar fashion but the end result is different. The glass on both was cleaned and the metal rods painted with spray paint, one done in a shiny chrome finish for a more modern look and the other in a pretty shade of blue. Both have sim-

ple off white fabric shades
adorned with purchased
trims– a textured flat
braid for the more mod-
ern one, and a gently
frilled trim for a romantic bedroom.

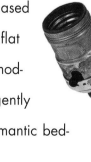

MATERIALS

- Sconces
- Masking tape
- Permanent marker
- Wire cutters
- Screwdriver
- Paint remover (like Zip Strip)
- Rubber gloves
- Dish soap
- Ammonia
- Old toothbrush
- White vinegar
- Chrome or glossy finish spray paint
- Craft glue
- Square-tipped artist's brush

FOR EACH LAMP
- 1 lamp socket with push switch
- 1 cord with attached plugs
- 1 purchased lamp shade
- Purchased trims or braid (enough to cover top and bottom edges of each shade)

1 Take the lamps apart by unscrewing the lock nut holding the threaded rods in place under the back section of the lamp. When you unscrew the socket as well, the lamp will start to separate into sections. Stick a piece of masking tape onto each piece and number sequentially with the marker, if needed. Cut though the old cords at the back of the lamps. Pull the old cord and socket through the lamp. Discard the old cords and sockets. [photo a]

2 Clean any rust off the metal pieces with steel wool, or apply paint remover to glass and metal rods, if needed, to remove old finish. Work in a well-ventilated space and wear a protective mask and rubber gloves. After 15 minutes the finish will start to soften. Wipe off as much of the old finish as you can with paper towels, then use an old toothbrush to remove the rest. Wash in dish soap and water. Rinse well and let everything dry. [photo a]

3 Spray the metal pieces with 2 or 3 coats of the chrome (or glossy) spray paint following the directions on the can, letting them dry between coats. When spray painting the

a

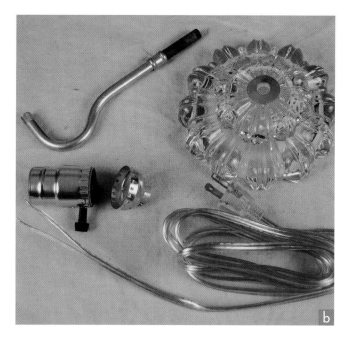

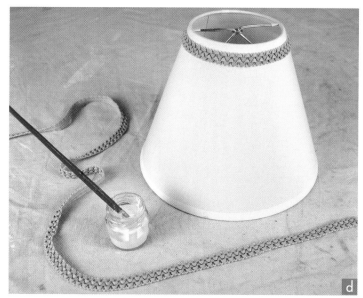

pieces, stick the numbered piece of masking tape in front of each piece on the paper before you spray paint it. Let dry completely. [photo b]

4 Clean all the glass pieces thoroughly inside and out using water with dish soap and a little ammonia added. Use the old toothbrush to scrub the dirt out of crevices. When everything is clean fill the sink with cool water. Add a small amount of white vinegar to the water and rinse the pieces carefully. Dry everything thoroughly. Reassemble the lamp and rewire the lamp following the directions on page 117. [photos c]

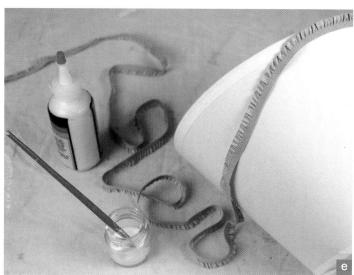

5 Trim the purchased shades following directions on page 130 for applying a decorative trim. [Photos d and e]

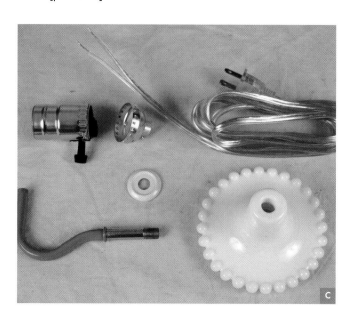

Distressed Column Lamps

These miniature Corinthian columns had acquired three different layers of paint by the time they came into my hands. Originally painted a dark tan, at some point they had also been painted white and then blue-green. The columns were nicely distressed, with some of the original wood showing through the layers of artfully peeling paint, almost as though they had sprung from some ancient ruin. To this day, I have no idea what their original purpose was, but I decided they would make great lamps.

Initially, their height was a drawback. It took me a while to find someone with the right length drill to make the opening for the threaded rod that extends through the lamp and to figure out how the base should be constructed. I'm really pleased with how I transformed the columns in the end. You can use this technique with any column or piece of turned wood, such as a banister or table leg. Even new ones could work: They can be painted like the bases to look old.

MATERIALS

- Wooden columns
- 4 basswood rosettes (2 small and 2 large)
- Wood glue
- Concentrated artist's acrylic in raw umber, raw sienna, aqua, green umber, titanium white (or colors of choice)
- Plastic dishes
- Small artist's brush or sea sponge
- Glaze medium
- Drill
- Pliers
- Wire cutter

FOR EACH LAMP
- 1 threaded rod/hex nut/lock washer/ check ring/bushing
- 2 vase caps (1 large and 1 small)
- 1 threaded brass neck
- 1 harp/harp bottom
- 1 lamp socket with three-way switch
- 1 cord set with attached plug
- Pressure-sensitive felt
- 1 lamp shade
- 1 lamp finial

1 Make a base for the column by centering the smaller wood rosette on top of the larger one. Glue them together with wood glue. Set them aside until the glue is dry. [photo a]

2 Squeeze a small amount of raw umber and raw sienna paint into a plastic dish. Use the sponge to dab both shades of paint separately onto the base, completely covering the surface in an irregular, mottled fashion. Let it dry.

3 On another plate, squeeze a small amount each of the aqua and green umber paint; mix each with a small amount of white paint and glaze medium to make two shades of light and dark aqua. Use the sponge to dab the two shades of paint onto the base, mottling irregularly. Let some of the under color show through. Let it dry. Apply another coat of mottled aqua paint if needed. Let it dry. (If you're starting from scratch with new columns, they can be painted in the same way, following all the steps above.) [photo b]

d

4 Drill or have a hole drilled through each column and the centers of the stacked bases wide enough to accommodate the threaded rod. On the underside of each base, using a 1⅛-inch drill bit, drill out the center hole three fourths of the way through the base. This will widen the center hole to accommodate the washer and nut that will hold the threaded rod in place.

5 Drill another hole through the side of the bottom section of the base parallel to the bottom edge of the base and centered from side to side and from top to bottom, all the way through the base, ending where it meets the vertical hole. The electrical cord will exit here, allowing the base to rest securely on a table.

6 Slip the check ring onto the threaded rod, then tighten with a lock washer and nut. Screw the bushing onto the bottom of the rod. Place the columns on the rosettes with the threaded rod extending up through both. This will help hold the column and base in place while the rest of the lamp is being assembled. [photo c]

7 Use the pliers to pull the threaded rod up through the columns and stack the two vase caps on the rod with the larger one on the bottom. Screw the brass neck onto the rod. Add the harp bottom and screw the socket base onto the threaded rod, tightening the socket base set screw. [photo d]

8 Insert the lamp cord through the hole in the side of the base and then up through the threaded rod and out the socket base. If the cord sticks going through the wood base, rub a little petroleum jelly on the outside covering of the cord, not on the end. Pull out some extra wire at the top so you have plenty to work with.

9 Split the wire and make an underwriter's knot if there is room in the cap. Strip the ends of each wire, exposing ½-inch of bare copper strands. Twist the strands of each wire tightly together, then wrap the neutral wire (covered with ridged insulation) clockwise around the silver terminal screw, tightening the screw securely over the loop. Wrap the smoother hot wire clockwise around the brass terminal and tighten. Snap the socket body in place and replace the insulating cardboard sleeve and the shell.

10 Press or glue a precut piece of pressure-sensitive felt to the bottom of the lamp. Attach the harp, place the lamp shade on top, and screw in the finial.

Tip for Making Bases

If you preferred, you could make, or have someone make for you, the base for the lamp out of a piece of hardwood. I was lucky to find these rosettes in two graduated sizes that worked with the diameter of the column to use as the base for the lamp. Look for them at a lumberyard or a store like Home Depot or Lowe's. They are part of the moldings that go into framing a door. I used rosettes made from basswood, but if I were doing it again I would probably choose hardwood, which costs more but is a little easier to work with. When working with the basswood, the drilling has to be done with care because though the wood is soft, it has a tendency to shred if you are not cautious.

Woven Paper Drum Shade

The woven paper lamp shade can be made from any heat-resistant, heavy card stock. I chose a heavy, smooth-surfaced printmaking paper; but you will find a varied selection of suitable papers at most art supply stores. A cylindrical shade like this is properly called a drum shade. It works very well with bases that have a clean, vertical shape.

MATERIALS

- 1 set of bottom and top lamp shade rings (with washer top fitting) of equal size
- Large sheet of heat-resistant, heavy card stock
- Soft lead pencil
- Clear plastic gridded ruler
- Craft knife
- Metal-edged ruler
- Cutting mat
- Masking tape
- Square-tipped artist's brush
- Craft glue
- Soft white eraser
- Clothespins
- Wax paper
- Small weights
- Double-fold bias tape to match card stock
- Compass
- Scissors

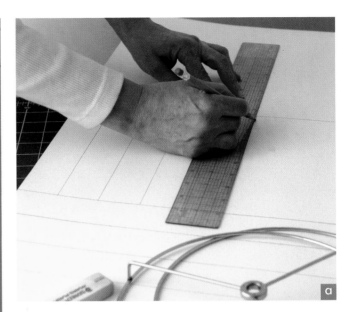

1 Measure the circumference of the rings and add 1 inch. Use this measurement to draw a rectangle on the card stock, with short sides corresponding to the height you want your lamp shade to be. Draw a second rectangle with the same dimensions above it on the card stock.

2 To make the horizontal strips, with the plastic ruler and pencil, lightly draw lines parallel to one rectangle's length at 1½-inch increments. You may need to adjust the measurements to fit your paper's dimensions, making sure to divide the paper into an odd number of strips. (Be sure the strips are at least 1 inch wide.)

3 To make the vertical strips, with the plastic ruler and pencil, lightly draw lines parallel to the other rectangle's width at 1½-inch increments. Adjust the measurements so the strips are the exact same width as the long strips above. [photo a]

4 With the craft knife and the metal-edged ruler, cut out the 2 rectangles. Cut each into strips, cutting along the pencil lines. [photo b]

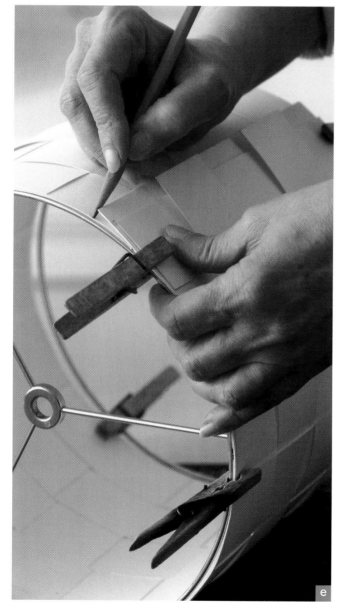

5 Align the vertical strips with the long edges parallel and touching on the cutting mat. Use the masking tape to secure the ends of the strips to the mat on one short side only. Weave the horizontal strips under and over the vertical ones, pushing them as tightly against each of the previous strips as possible until they are all used. Remove the tape. [photo c]

6 With the small brush, apply glue to the ends of the strips where they overlap all along the outside edges. Press together and let dry for an hour. Turn the woven paper rectangle over and repeat on the other side. Again, let dry completely before proceeding. Erase any pencil marks left on the card stock. [photo d]

7 Hold the bottom (spokeless) ring in one hand. place the bottom center front of the woven paper rectangle on the wire ring and clamp the edge to the ring with a clothespin. Following the natural curve of the paper, fit the shade around the ring, fastening it as you go with the clothespins. Work first toward the left until you reach the outside edge. Return to the center front and fit the right half of the shade to the ring. Repeat for the top ring. Adjust the fit so the top and bottom of the shade fit evenly around the edge of the rings and there are no gaps: There will be approximately a ½-inch overlap where the back seam edges meet. With the back seam facing you, lightly mark the top and bottom seam overlap. [photo e]

8 Remove the clothespins and set the rings aside. Place the shade on the cutting mat with the right side faceup. Use the straightedge if necessary to trim the overlap to ½-inch. Turn the shade over and with the wrong side faceup apply a thin, even coat of glue along the entire length of the back seam overlap, keeping within the imaginary line indicating the inside edge of the seam allowance. Lifting the edge of the shade, hold it so the right side is facing you and apply a thin, even coat along the entire length of the seam allowance on the outside (right side). [photo f]

9 Bending the shade into shape, line up the top edge along the pencil mark and fasten with a clothespin. Secure the bottom edge in the same fashion. Hold the glued seam together for a few minutes until the glue sets, then place, seam-side down, on a piece of wax paper. Remove the clothespins and place small weights along the back seam. Let dry for 15 to 20 minutes, removing the weights when the glue is completely dry.

10 Stand the shade on the work surface with the top resting on the table. With the brush, apply a thin line of glue along the bottom inside edge of the shade, rotating the shade as you work. Ease the bottom ring into place starting at the center front, positioning the weld in the ring slightly to the right of the back seam. Fasten the ring in place with the clothespins, making sure the ring is positioned evenly inside the shade. Repeat with the top ring, positioning one of the top ring's 3 spokes in line with the back seam of the shade. Let the glue dry for 20 minutes and then remove the clothespins. [photo g]

11 To bind the top and bottom edges of the shade to the wire rings, use a trim such as double-fold bias tape. Draw a guideline around the top and bottom edge using the ruler or a compass. Cut a piece of binding to fit the top edge of the shade and square off one end of the binding. Starting at the squared end, apply glue to the lower half of the first few inches. Press the binding into place, starting ¼-inch to the left of the back seam and just covering the marked line. Allow the glue to set for a minute. Continue to apply the

glue to the lower half of the binding, working in 9- to 10-inch segments, holding the binding away from the shade. Press the binding in place as before, making sure it is smooth and even. Continue until you reach the back seam. Using the back seam as a guide, trim the binding perpendicular to the edge of the shade. Apply glue to the full width of the binding at the back seam. Overlap the edges and press into place. [photo h]

12 On the top ring only, use the scissors to make small slashes in the binding where the spokes connect to the wire ring. Apply a thin, even coat of glue to the inside half of the binding and press in place to the inside of the shade, rolling and molding the binding over the top of the wire. Turning the shade on its side, reach inside the shade and use your fingernail to crease the edge of the binding around the wire. Repeat for the bottom edge, omitting the slashes for the spokes.

Binding for Shades

Other popular bindings for lamp shades are ⅝-inch grosgrain ribbon or cotton twill tape. Polyester ribbons should be avoided, as they repel glue. Different kinds of decorative braids can also be used, though on a busy shade a simple trim is more effective. On a solid-color fabric shade a binding made with the same fabric would be preferable.

Picking Shade Materials

Many heavy papers and fabrics make unique lamp shades. To preview how it will look, hold the paper or fabric up to a lightbulb. You will be able to see immediately if the paper or fabric works well under the light. Look for fabric that is evenly woven with no slubs or knots (unless it is a slubbed silk, which is meant to be that way). Printed fabric or paper should be consistently colored, not blotchy. With textured papers eliminate any that have uneven thick and thin areas that will show up when the light is on. Make sure to ask a salesperson whether your choice of paper is heat resistant.

Chairs and Tables

've always found it easy to ferret out worn but charming chairs and benches at thrift stores, especially the bigger ones that offer an extensive selection of furniture. Among my favorite finds were a dark green velvet boudoir chair with a down-stuffed seat cushion, a classic fifties lounge chair in chartreuse green Naugahyde, a couple of quirky benches, and numerous wooden dining room and kitchen chairs. The velvet chair was slightly worn but still far from shabby and it had an air of fading glamour, as if it had once dwelt in the bedroom of an old romantic Hollywood movie. The fifties chair is exactly like those I've seen since selling for much more in tony retro furniture stores.

Even better bargains were the chairs I've found free for the taking in Dumpsters or trash piles. People frequently discard old wooden kitchen type chairs when all they really need are some simple repairs. I've often rescued slightly broken chairs from the trash in order to reconstruct them. Basic repairs are very easy to accomplish; usually the joints on the legs or sides will need to be reglued. If you take the time to thoroughly clean the joints before regluing and allow the glue to dry thoroughly, you can easily return the chair to working order, making it ready to strip or paint as you choose.

Wooden chairs are the easiest to make over—all it really takes to transform them is a few coats of paint. They have the advantage of being easy to repaint if you decide to change your color scheme. Cane seats can be painted over as well. For an antique look, the finish can be slightly distressed. Adding matching upholstered seats or cushions, in addition to the paint, can tie different shapes together. This way a variety of chairs can bring a creative edge to a dining room or kitchen table without looking too disorganized. I personally find using different shapes of chairs much more fun than a traditional matching set.

As for upholstered pieces, you should keep your eye out for two kinds of finds: fine, well-made pieces and not so well-made but pleasing and useful pieces. A good quality, well-made piece of upholstered furniture is always worth buying, even if you can't stand the fabric. The cost of restoring and/or recovering is generally far less than the cost of a comparable new piece. Sometimes you'll come across a pleasant and useful piece but one that's not particularly well made —the workmanship is so-so, the materials of inferior quality. Even so, it can be worth buying and refurbishing on the cheap—until you can replace it with something better. I have one upholstered club chair that I bought for $35; it had a nice shape and was very comfortable but was covered in the most awful cheap fabric and was definitely not a good piece of furniture. But I had a slipcover made for it and it looks just fine—as a matter of fact, I've always regretted not buying the matching one.

Small tables are another element I've used time and time again—they function both as useful surfaces and decorative touches. They can be especially useful when entertaining—as a second bar area or an additional surface for hors d'oeuvres. Use the top of a small table to show off a collection or improvise a work area in front of a sunny window. The top of a smallish table provides a neat flat surface for bringing a bold splash of color or pattern and providing instant personality for the piece. And if the table is a small one it will not dominant the setting but enliven the surrounding space.

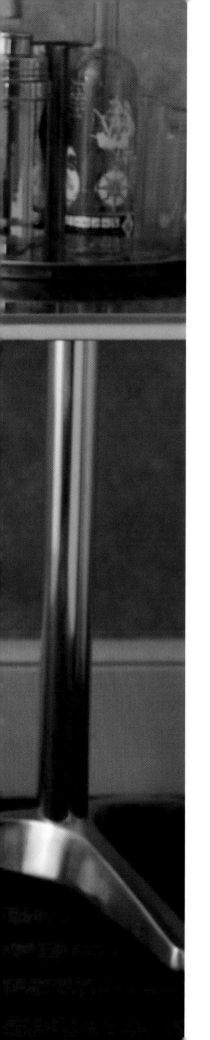

Metal Office Chair

Old metal office furniture, especially pieces that have been stripped down to the base metal, have become much in demand. But you can still find unrefinished pieces like this desk chair at bargain prices. The traditional, romantic toile fabric contrasts stylishly with the sleek metal, an unexpected combination of two disparate elements that works. You can re-cover the chair yourself but I would suggest sending the piece out to be reupholstered as re-covering metal furniture requires slightly different methods than those used on a more traditional piece because the under part is metal. In this case, the cost of having the chair professionally re-covered seemed very reasonable as the chair initially cost only $5 at the Salvation Army.

MATERIALS

- Metal desk chair
- Screwdriver
- Paint remover (like Zip Strip)
- Rubber gloves
- Protective mask
- Household paintbrush
- Putty knife
- Steel wool
- Power drill with medium wire brush wheel
- Spray lacquer
- Black and white toile fabric
- ¼-inch plywood (optional)

1 Take the upholstered seat and armrests off the chair by removing the screws that hold them in place from the underside of the metal frame. The backrest is held in place with screws also, but it has metal tabs on the backside as well that slide into slots on the top edge of the frame. Remove the screws first, then the backrest can drop down and out of the frame. Set the upholstered pieces aside. [photo a]

2 Remove the paint from the frame with paint remover, following the directions on the container. Scrape off old paint with the putty knife. Make sure to work outside or in a well-ventilated space and wear a protective mask, if needed. Any stubborn areas can be gone over with steel

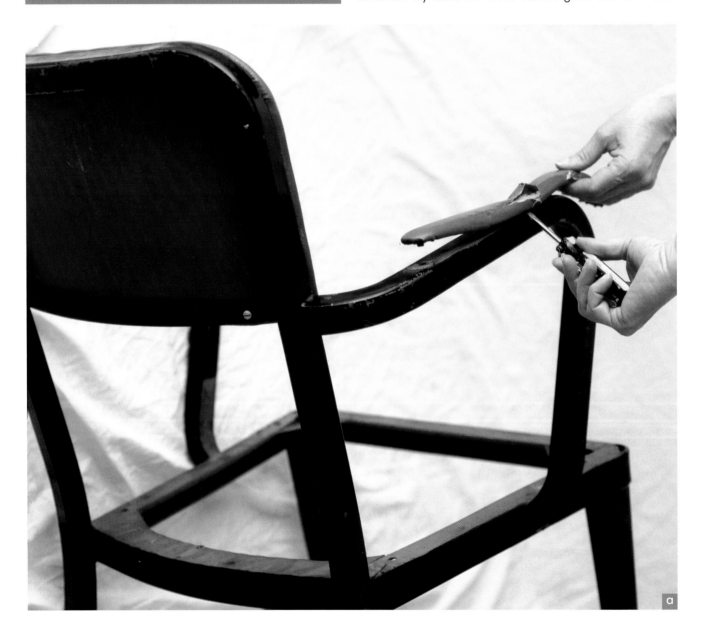

a

b

Stripping and Polishing Metal Furniture

Working on one small section (like a leg) at a time, apply paint remover. Work outside or in a well-ventilated space and wear a protective mask. After 15 minutes the paint will start to soften and appear crinkled. Scrape off as much of the softened paint as you can with a putty knife, then use a medium-grade steel wool pad to remove the rest. Discard the pad when it fills up with paint. If necessary, apply a second coat of paint remover and repeat the process. Attach a medium steel wire brush to a power drill and work slowly and evenly over the surface of the frame. Finish smoothing and polishing the surface, working evenly back and forth across the frame to achieve an overall brushed, satin finish. Be sure to keep the drill moving over the frame to ensure a uniform-looking brushed pattern. Wipe down with a clean cloth and spray with clear satin lacquer if desired.

wool. Polish the frame using the power drill with a wire brush attachment to give the metal a brushed finish. When you have achieved the desired finish, spray the frame with lacquer to protect it. [photo b]

3 Make new covers for the seat, backrest, and armrests by taking them apart to use as patterns for the new covers. The original padding can usually be reused. One tip that will help: Cut a new bottom for the drop-in chair seat out of ¼-inch-thick plywood to replace the existing metal seat bottom. Alternatively, bring the upholstered pieces—and the frame—to an upholsterer to have the pieces re-covered and the chair reassembled. If you do want to give it a try yourself, consult a good reference book on upholstery techniques. [photo c]

c

Wooden Kitchen Chair

I spotted this chair on the curb one night and of course stopped to pick it up. The sole survivor of a vintage forties kitchen set, the chair's attractive architecturally shaped back was still apparent beneath the many layers of paint acquired over the years. Because chairs from this period are so sturdy, my dumpster find was basically in excellent shape. For the cushion, I chose scraps of vintage floral; the soft creaminess of the paint picks up the creamy tones in the flowers and leaves in a very pleasing way.

MATERIALS

- Wooden chair
- Power sander (optional)
- Sandpaper
- Paint remover (Like Zip Strip)
- Primer
- Household paintbrush
- Satin finish oil-based paint
- Soft lead pencil
- Clear plastic gridded ruler
- Brown paper
- Scissors
- Printed cotton fabric
- Solid-color twill fabric
- Pins
- Sewing machine
- Cotton sewing thread
- ½-inch cotton cording
- Household Iron
- ½-inch-thick foam cushion insert
- Hand sewing needle

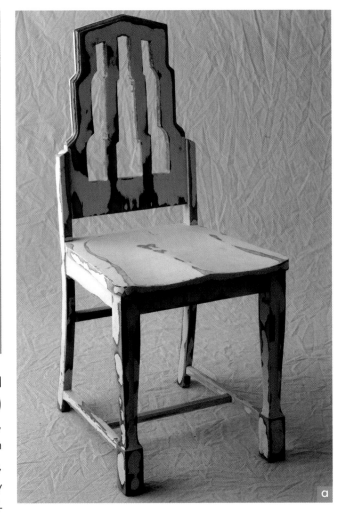

1 If the existing layers of paint are especially thick, sand the chair with the power sander (make sure to wear a mask) to remove some of the paint and create an even, smooth, nonglossy surface. Alternatively, remove the paint with paint remover. If you choose to remove the paint entirely, prime with primer and when dry, sand the surface lightly with fine-grade sandpaper. Paint with 2 coats of the oil-based satin finish paint. Let dry completely. [photo a]

2 To make a pattern for the chair cushion, place a piece of brown paper on the seat and outline the edges with a soft lead pencil. [photo b]

3 Remove the paper pattern and with the ruler and pencil draw a vertical line down its center. Fold the pattern in half along that line, with the traced outline facing out. Working on one half, straighten out the lines. Leave the paper folded in half and cut around the new line with scissors. Unfold the pattern and lay on the chair seat to check, making any adjustments. [photo c]

4 Place the pattern on the printed fabric and carefully center the motif; secure with pins. Cut out the top cushion cover. Cut out the bottom cushion cover from the solid-color fabric. Make up the piping as follows: Find the cross grain or bias

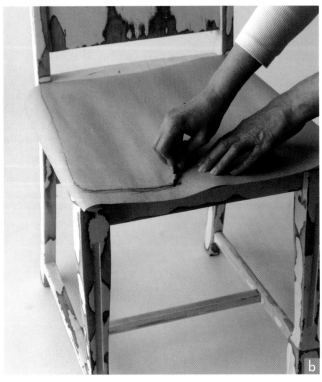

by folding a corner of the solid fabric up to the opposite selvage in a triangle. The fold will form a 45-degree angle to the selvage. The line formed by the fold is the bias or cross grain of the fabric. With a pencil, mark parallel lines starting at the fold at 1½-inch intervals on the solid fabric. Cut enough 1½-inch-wide-bias strips to fit around the chair cushion and to make 4 chair ties.

5 To join the bias strips together, cut the ends at a right angle and overlap the 2 ends, right sides together at right (90-degree) angles to each other. Machine stitch across the diagonal, trim off the corner, and press open. Repeat with

the other strips until you have enough to fit around the cushion. To make the piping, lay the cord in the center of the wrong side of the bias strip and fold in half. Using a zipper foot, machine stitch as close to the cord as possible. Make the cushion ties out of four 18-inch-long strips of bias. Turn the raw edges to the inside and top stitch on the right side.

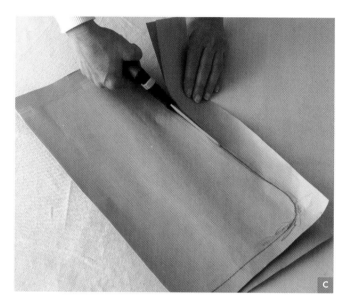

6 With the raw edges together, pin the piping to the right side of the bottom cushion cover and machine stitch, allowing a ½-inch seam allowance. Sew 2 chair ties into the seam allowance at each back corner at the same time. Snip the piping seam allowance around the curves and when turning the corners allow the piping to lay flat. [photo d]

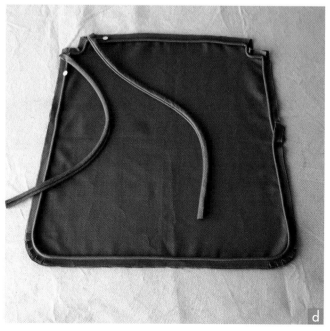

7 Lay the top cushion cover underneath the bottom with the right sides together and machine stitch following the previous stitching line, leaving an opening in the back to insert the pad. Trim the fabric at the corners, turn right side out, and press. Insert the foam cushion into the cushion cover and hand-sew the opening closed using a needle and cotton thread to match. Knot the exposed end of each chair tie and trim the raw edge as close to the knot as possible. [photo e]

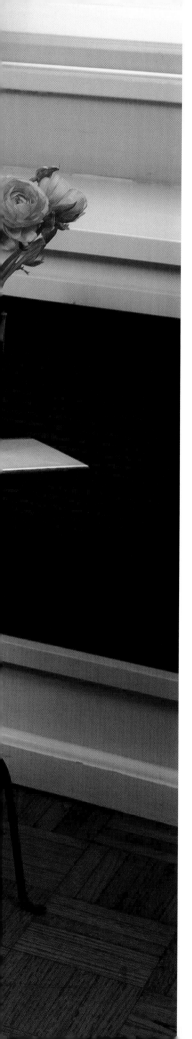

Fifties Lounge Chair

Chairs like this one turn up occasionally in second hand or thrift stores. The original covering was vinyl and was in such bad shape I stripped it off shortly after I found the piece. The exposed legs and back supports were covered with a dark stain of some sort. Refinshing them was quite simple as both the legs and the seat back are easily unbolted from the frame. After removing the old finish I stained the legs and back supports with a teak wood stain that brought out the warm tones in the wood. I decided to take the chair to be up-holstered at a shop as it needed all new padding and the large scale pattern I wanted to use needed to be carefully fitted.

MATERIALS

- Upholstered chair
- Adjustable wrench
- Pliers
- Rubber gloves
- Protective mask
- Paint remover (like Zip-Strip)
- Household paint brush
- Fine-grade steel wool
- Fine-grade sandpaper
- or sanding sponge
- Cheesecloth
- Oil- based wood stain (here Zar in Teak Natural)
- Polyurethane or tung oil
- Fabric of your choice (here Josef Frank's Hawaii)

1 Remove the back from the seat, turn seat over and unbolt the legs from the frame. Put all the nuts and bolts aside for later. I like to put them in a zip-lock bag and label the outside of the bag using a permanent market.

2 Working on one leg at a time, apply the paint remover following the directions on the container. Work in a well-ventilated space and wear a protective mask and rubber gloves. After 15 minutes the finish will start to soften. [photo a]

3 Wipe off as much of the old finish as you can with paper towels, then use a fine-grade steel wool pad to remove the rest. If necessary, apply a second coat of paint remover and repeat the process. Do the same with the exposed wood on the upright back supports. Sand lightly if needed. Wipe down well before applying stain.

4 With a pad of cheesecloth, liberally apply the wood stain working on one piece at a time, following the directions on the container. Allow the stain to penetrate the surface no longer then 3 to 5 minutes. [photo b]

5 While the stain is still wet, use another section of the cheesecloth pad to wipe off the excess, working in the direction of the wood grain. Continue until all the legs and the upright back supports are stained. Set them aside to dry. If

a deeper color is desired, an additional application of stain may be applied after the first coat is dry. Let dry, then sand lightly if needed and finish with polyurethane or tung oil.

6 When they are completely dry reattach the stained legs to the underside of the seat frame and the stained upright back supports to the back of the seat frame. [photo c and d]

7 Make new covers for the seat and back. If you have the original coverings they can be taken apart and used as patterns for the new covers. Sometimes the original padding can be reused, as well. Alternatively, bring the frame to an upholsterer to have a new cover made and in this case I had to have new padding added as well. If you do want to give it a try yourself, consult a good reference book on upholstery techniques.

Carved Wooden Armchair

Some friends arrived at a birthday party for my husband Vince, with this large wooden armchair in tow. Their longtime neighbors had been about to discard it after many years as the patriarch's "special chair." Our friends felt this chair, owing to its long history, deserved a new home where it would be appreciated. While I'm not quite sure that the gentleman would recognize his beloved armchair today —painted white and recovered in this lustrous blue striped Thai silk—I think he would be glad to see that it is still a much loved spot for reading and contemplation.

MATERIALS

- Wooden armchair
- Pliers
- Screwdriver
- Paint remover (like Zip Strip)
- Fine-grade steel wool
- Benjamin Moore Fresh Start Primer
- Fine-grade sandpaper
- Household paintbrush
- Satin finish water-based paint
- Fabric of your choice (enough to cover your piece

1 Carefully strip the original fabric covering and the underlying layers of padding off the frame or bring to an upholsterer and have him or her remove all the materials. If you want to strip the frame yourself, consult a good book on upholstery techniques. [photo a]

2 The stripped-down frame can now be painted or refinished. Rub down with fine-grade steel wool before painting if you don't want to remove the original finish. Clean the surface thoroughly, then prime with primer. Sand the surface lightly with fine-grade sandpaper or rub down with fine-grade steel wool. Apply 2 coats of satin finish paint, letting it dry completely between coats and after the final coat. [photo b]

3 The chair is now ready to be re-covered with the new fabric. If you are doing this yourself, again, use a good reference book on upholstery. If you are working with an upholsterer, bring the chair to the shop after it is painted and completely dry along with all the materials and layers of padding that have been previously removed.

NEW LIFE FOR SPRUNG UPHOLSTERED PIECES

The lovely, slightly faded green velvet on this chair was still in good condition but the webbing under the seat had completely given out and the springs underneath needed to be retied and attached to the frame. Rather than completely reupholster the piece I decided to dismantle the chair just enough to reach the springs and repair them. To gain access to the springs I needed first to completely remove the covering and padding on the lower part of the chair. Here's how to do it yourself: Using the end of a screwdriver, tap against the tacks to loosen them; you'll then be able to pull the tacks out with pliers. Working slowly, remove all of the old covering and padding with care, preserving everything for later reuse. [photo c]

After the lower part of the frame is completely stripped the new webbing can be stretched across the underside of the seat using a webbing stretcher, which creates the necessary tension. Start by placing the free end of the new webbing over the frame so that the end extends about an inch beyond the frame. Tack the webbing to the frame with four tacks. Fold the short end back on itself and tack again through both layers in three places. Using the stretcher, stretch the webbing across the frame, hold it down and attach it to the other side of the frame with four tacks. Trim the end allowing an inch beyond the tacks; fold the end back on itself. Follow the spacing of the original webbing and repeat the process from back to front across the frame and then from one side to the other side weaving the webbing over and under the vertical pieces as you go. [photo d]

With the firm base of the new webbing in place the springs are now ready to be retied. [photo e]

Eames Side Chair

house and knew that it could be easily stripped down to the original wood, which was likely to be birch. My parents had two original Eames chairs in birch similar to these, but with metal legs. This one looked like an original Eames also. I wanted to add something to it so decided to stencil a pattern on it. These large letters—in Helvetica, of course– were made on the computer and printed out on regular paper first. Then I printed them on adhesive-backed sheets transparent film to make stencils once I was happy with the size and arrangement.

MATERIALS

- All wood chair
- Paint remover (like Zip- Strip)
- Household paint brush
- Rubber gloves
- Protective mask
- Putty knife
- Paper towels
- Synthetic steel wool pad
- Fine-grade sandpaper or sanding sponge
- Mineral spirits
- Computer and photo and design program
- Printer and paper
- Painter's tape
- Clear adhesive-backed ink jet transparent plastic sheets
- Small sharp scissors
- Metal straight edge ruler
- Craft knife and mat
- Oil- based wood stain (here Zar in Teak Natural)
- Cheesecloth
- Polyurethane or tung oil

1 Working on one small section at a time, apply paint remover following the directions on the container. Work outside or in a well-ventilated space and wear a protective mask and rubber gloves. [photo a]

2 After 15 minutes the paint will start to soften and appear crinkled. Scrape off as much of the softened paint as you can with a putty knife, then use paper towels and a synthetic steel wool pad to remove the rest. If necessary, apply a second coat of paint remover and repeat the process. Clean piece with mineral spirits and sand the surfaces lightly. Wipe down. [photo b]

3 Choose a typeface for your letters or word (here I used Helvetica). Make each letter as large as you can in your word program, then using a photo or design program, enlarge them to the sizes needed, keeping each letter in the original proportions. I enlarged the letters used here as follows: "e"–5-inches, "a"–4-inches, "m"–6½-inches, "s"–9-inches, and smaller "e"–3¾-inches. Save the letter files and test the size and placement by printing

each out on regular white printer paper. Roughly cut them out and arrange on the piece until you pleased. Temporarily tape them in place. [photo c]

4 To make the stencils: print each enlarged letter on one adhesive-backed plastic sheet. Add bridges or connectors to each letter using strips of painter's tape, carefully planning where they belong on each stencil. Cut out the inside of the letters (the black spaces) carefully leaving the connectors intact by cutting around them. Cut out the shapes using a straight edge and craft knife for the straight lines and a small scissors for the curved lines. It is easier sometimes to turn the shapes rather then the moving the scissors on the curved edges. [photo d]

5 Working on one letter at a time remove the test letters and replace with the stencils. Firmly burnish the inside and outside letter edges on each stencil so they adhere to the surface of the chair. With a pad of cheesecloth, carefully apply the wood stain working on one letter at a time, following the directions on the container. Allow the stain to penetrate the surface no longer then 3 to 5 minutes. While the stain is still wet, use another section of the cheesecloth pad to wipe off the excess, working in the direction of the wood grain. If a deeper color is desired, an additional application of stain may be applied. Let dry and carefully remove the stencil. [photo e]

6 If there are a few small blotches they can be carefully cleaned up using the tip the craft knife. When the stain has completely dried on all the letters a finish coat of polyure-thane or tung oil can be applied following the directions on the container.

Console
Table

I'd always wanted a table in my dining room to provide some extra serving space. But I revised my idea when I came across these large, ornately carved brackets. They appear to be supporting the table but in reality the piece is hung on the wall as one unit. The top is made from new birch plywood and the wide carved molding is the type used on mantelpieces. I painted an old mirror to match and hung it just above the shelf surface at eye level. But I think it would look just as good with a framed picture and two sconces hanging on either side of the picture. Brackets like those shown here are often available from stores that specialize in architectural salvage. You may be able to find something less ornate but similar at a building supply store.

MATERIALS

- Wood brackets
- ½-inch plywood with birch veneered face
- Miter box with saw (optional)
- 4-inch-wide bolection or mantel molding
- Wood glue
- Finishing nails
- Clamp
- Hammer
- Wood putty
- Small weights
- Fine-grade sandpaper
- Benjamin Moore Fresh Start primer
- Satin finish interior paint
- 3- and 4-inch wood screws

1 The top of this table measures 13 x 38 inches. These measurements can be adjusted to fit the depth of your brackets and the width of your space. The depth of the top does not have to match the depth of the brackets exactly and can be adjusted to fit your needs and space considerations. After you decide on the size of your top, cut 2 pieces of plywood to those measurements. Cut 3 pieces of the molding, 1 for the front edge and 2 for the sides, to those measurements, mitering both corners on the front piece and only one corner on the side pieces, and cutting the other end straight across. The lumberyard should be able to cut these pieces as well as the plywood for you. [photo a]

b

2 Make a box that is open in the back by attaching the molding to the plywood bottom and top. Glue the side pieces of the molding in place along the lower and top edges of the plywood with the wood glue. Secure the molding further with finishing nails. Cut 2 pieces of scrap plywood to fit inside the box, gluing each one vertically on the inside between the top and bottom pieces to provide some additional support for the top. Clamp the molding to hold it in place until the glue sets. Glue the front piece of molding in place along the top and bottom edges, making sure to use plenty of glue at the 2 mitered corners. Wipe any excess glue away with a damp cloth or paper towel. Clamp until the glue sets. Secure the molding further with finishing nails. Recess all the nails using a punch or another nail.

3 Fill any spaces or gaps along the edges or nail holes in the molding with wood putty. Place the top, face side down, on a smooth surface and mark the position of the brackets, placing them 6 to 8 inches in from the sides. Glue the brackets to the un-

derside of the top with the wood glue. Clamp or place weights on the brackets until the glue sets and is completely dry. Sand the piece lightly and prime everything, including the brackets, with the primer. Paint with 2 coats of the satin finish interi paint, letting the paint dry between coats. Let dry completely. [photo b]

4 To hang the unit on the wall, attach 2 small blocks of wood to the wall at the desired height (I hung this at counterheight, 36 inches from the floor to the top). The blocks should be narrow enough so that the opening in the back of the table is able to slip over them but deep enough to provide support to the table, which will rest on top of the blocks: I used two 4-inch lengths of a 2 x 4. Anchor the blocks firmly into the wall beams with 4-inch-long wood screws so they can support the weight of the table. Slip the unit over the blocks and drill holes downward through the tabletop into each block in 2 places. Screw into place with 3-inch-long wood screws. Recess the screw heads and fill the holes with wood putty. If there is a large gap between the table and the wall it can be filled in with caulk and painted to match.

Choosing Stock Molding

Many different kinds, sizes, and shapes of stock moldings are available. For the best selection seek out the stores or catalogs that offer specialty moldings—you will find a wider and more interesting range to choose from. Moldings can be used individually as here, or stacked one on top of another to produce a more elaborate effect. Visit a historical home or period room in a museum to see how moldings are used in the mantels and fireplace surrounds, for chair or picture rails, or to create detailing on doors and embellish windows.

Combed Table

Small odd tables like this are a stylish alternative to a coffee table. You can group two or three together for a larger surface area or scatter them around a room. They don't take up very much space and are light enough to be moved frequently. Their scale makes them the perfect companion for a small couch like the one here or in a smaller room where space is limited. They are fairly easy to find at flea markets or house sales. I found this one at a small flea market in upstate New York. In this room it needed to be painted a strong color to stand up to the floral pattern on the couch, but I've seen a similar table painted antique white and it looked equally nice.

MATERIALS

- Small wooden table
- Sandpaper
- Lighter color satin fin-
  ish water-based paint
- Small foam paint roller
- Colored pencil to
  match deeper shade
  paint
- Ruler
- Painter's tape
- Craft knife

- Water-based glaze
  medium
- Concentrated artist's
  acrylic paint in deeper
  shade
- Small household
  paintbrush
- Combing tool
- Artist's brush
- Matte finish varnish

1 Sand the table as much as necessary to achieve a smooth surface and remove any old, flaking paint. Paint with 2 coats (letting dry between coats) of the satin finish water-based paint. Let dry completely. Using the colored pencil and the ruler, divide the tabletop into 3-inch squares, marking them lightly on the surface of the table. [photo a]

2 Using the painter's tape, mark off rows of alternate squares. These squares will be painted and combed first. [photo b]

3 Mix one part glaze medium with one part of the artist's acrylic paint. For the horizontal squares, use the small paintbrush to apply the tinted glaze with even, horizontal brush strokes to one square at a time. [photo c]

4 Starting at the left edge, drag the comb from left to right through the tinted glaze. For even lines, drag the comb in one fluid movement. If the glaze smudges, smooth out with the paintbrush add a little more of the tinted glaze and try again. Wipe the combing tool after each square to remove excess glaze. [photo d]

5 Let the squares dry completely and then remove the tape. [photo e]

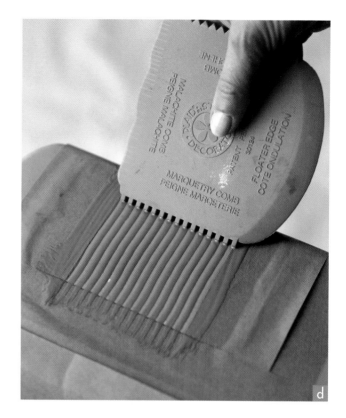

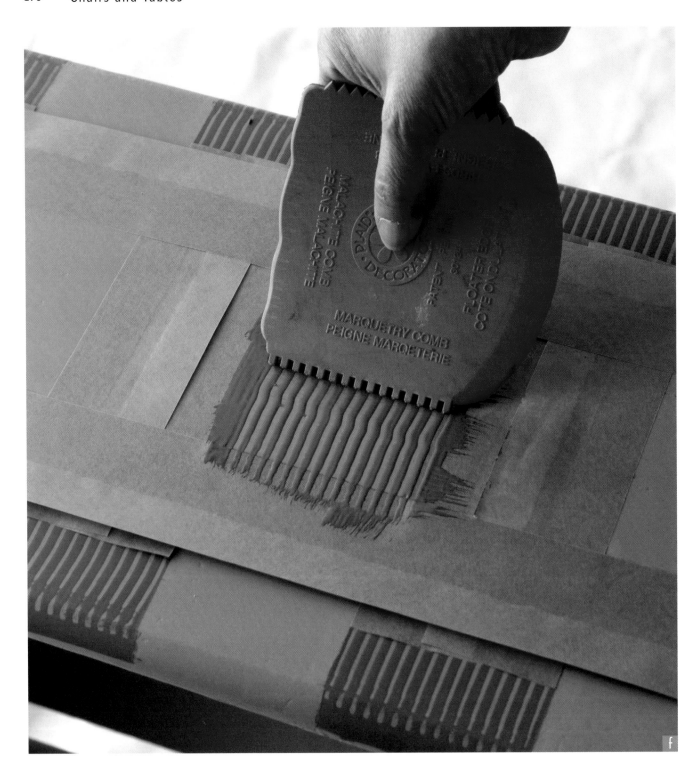

6 Repeat the taping, painting, and combing for alternate rows of horizontal squares. [photo f]

7 When completely dry, remove the old tape and using the painter's tape, mark off the vertical squares that do not touch along alternate rows. Working on one square at a time as before, apply the glaze with even vertical brush strokes, but this time start at the top of the square and drag the comb down to the bottom. Let dry completely and then remove the tape. Repeat the process for the remaining vertical squares. [photo g]

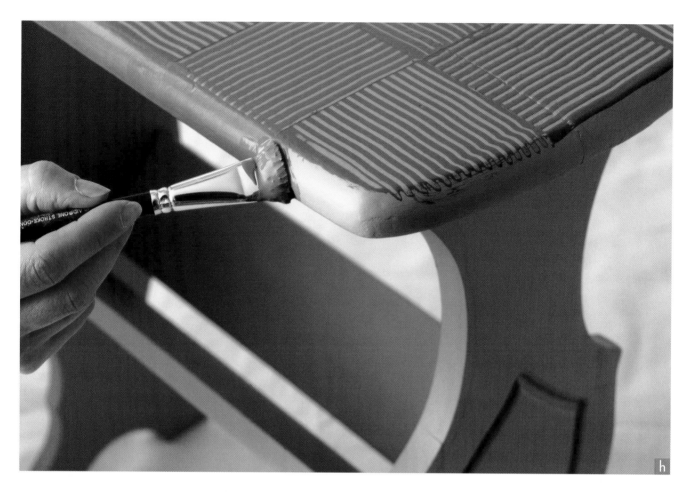

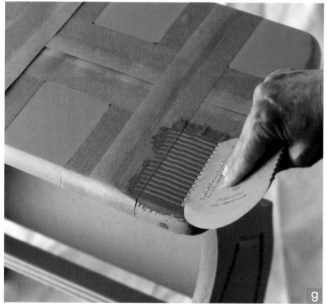

How to Make a Combing Tool

Different-sized combing tools can be purchased, but they are easy to make yourself to suit the scale of your project. For a larger project, grooves can be cut in a window washer's squeegee with a craft knife. A piece of sturdy cardboard works well as a temporary combing tool for a smaller project. It will wear out more quickly than a rubber one, so plan your use accordingly. Experiment with the size and spacing of the grooves until you are satisfied with the results.

8 Using the artist's paintbrush and the tinted glaze, hand paint the edge of the table to give it a finished look. Let dry. Apply 2 coats of matte varnish to the tabletop to finish. [photo h]

Folding
Card Table

My father had this table in his basement for many years and was about to consign it to the trash one day when I happened to be visiting. I was immediately drawn to the floral image on the top and so took it home with the intention of taking the cardboard top off and framing it. It sat around for a long time before I looked at it again. And when I did, I happened to need an extra table for a special occasion. I decided that it was really a very useful and sweet little table to have. It folds out of the way when you don't need it and can be used in any number of ways and for a multitude of tasks such as impromptu dining indoors or out, an extra work surface, and even for its original use as a card table.

MATERIALS

- Folding table
- Wood saw
- ⅛-inch medium-density fiberboard
- Wood glue
- Wood dowel
- Sandpaper
- Small paintbrush
- Water-based wood stain
- Cheesecloth or clean rag
- Ruler
- Scissors
- Artist's linen
- Household iron
- Fusible web
- Soft lead pencil
- Masking tape in two widths: ½-inch and 1½-inch
- Concentrated artist's paint in complementary colors
- Small dish
- Stenciling brush
- Small finishing nails

1 Remove the original cardboard tabletop from the table frame and use it as a pattern to cut a new top out of ⅛-inch fiberboard. Set both aside. [photo a]

2 Inspect the table frame and legs for any missing pieces (mine was missing a dowel) or loose joints. Remove any loose nails and reglue the corners using wood glue. Apply glue liberally to the joint and press the 2 sides together. Wipe excess glue away from the joint with a clean cloth. Renail the corners of the frame together if necessary. Let the glue dry completely. I also cut a length of dowel to replace the missing piece and glued it in place.

3 If needed, use a wood refinishing product or paint stripper to remove the old finish. Here a light sanding was enough and removed the little bit of finish that was left.

4 With the small paintbrush, liberally apply the water-based stain, working on a small area at a time, following the directions on the container. Allow the stain to penetrate the surface no longer than 3 to 5 minutes. [photo b]

5 While the stain is still wet, use a piece of cheese-cloth or clean soft rag to wipe off the excess, working in the direction of the wood grain. Continue until frame is completely stained. Set frame aside. [photo c]

6 Make the new fabric-covered top as follows: Measure the fiberboard top and cut a piece of artist's linen to those dimensions, adding 2 inches to each side for turning. Iron the fusible web to the wrong side of the fabric, following the manufacturer's directions. Center the fabric, right-side up and fusibles-side down, on the fiberboard top. Trim the excess fabric by cutting triangles of the linen ½-inch away from the fiberboard corners. Again following directions, use the iron to fuse the fabric to the board. Turn over and wrap the excess fabric to the back of the board; fuse in place as before.

7 Decide on the width of the 2 stripes to be painted on the tabletop. Here the narrow stripe is ¼-inch wide and the wide stripe is 1½-inches wide. Either draw directly on the canvas with a pencil to mark the lines for the stripes or use the width of the masking tape itself as a measure.

8 Measure the border area that will remain unpainted and mask it off with 1 or 2 rows of masking tape. Mark the space for the narrow stripe by laying down a line of the ¼-inch masking tape around the perimeter of the previously masked-off border. This narrow band of masking tape can then be removed when you are ready to paint the narrower stripe. Mask off the areas on either side of the wider stripe that will not be painted with strips of the masking tape to protect them while you are painting the ½-inch stripe. [photo d]

Pour a small amount of the first paint into a dish. Using the stencil brush, daub the paint onto the canvas, completely covering the wider stripe with the paint. When the paint is dry, remove the ¼-inch-wide masking tape to expose the unpainted canvas for the narrower stripe. Pour a small amount of the second color of paint in a dish. Carefully daub the second paint onto the canvas, completely covering the narrow stripe. When the paint is completely dry, remove all the remaining masking tape. [photos e and f]

10 Place the finished top on the base and attach with small finishing nails.

Simple Storage

We all know that you can never have too much storage space, but what you may not realize is that creating order in your home can be a stylish process as well. In my family, everyone has about twenty different hobbies and interests, and it's a creative challenge to keep our home from feeling disordered and cluttered. Having everything you need in one place—like writing paper and pens on your desk—eliminates unnecessary stress by streamlining the functions of a space. If you start by assessing where and what kind of storage each room needs, you can look for reasonably priced pieces that will bring a sense of order to that ever expanding clutter. Old pieces can be turned to new uses—like a metal vegetable bin used to store towels—and decorated to fit in with the space so that they become attractive additions as well. Use your imagination to create storage opportunities.

For many years, even after our son, Alex, was born, my husband and I lived in a tiny apartment. We were forced to be relentlessly creative about storage—everything was scrutinized for its usefulness and anything extraneous banished (this was long before my days of rescuing other people's castoffs). Everything in that apartment had its place just like the living quarters of a ship. Now our constant challenge is to contain all of our interests and collections with the added space of a house. We always seem to be in need of more bookshelves for housing all our books and a growing number of CDs, for displaying collections of glass and pottery, for keeping art and craft supplies accessible.

Bookcases really are the most versatile kind of storage space. I have at least one in almost every room of my house that I use for a range of purposes, from storing games in my son's room to showcasing a collection of pottery in the dining room, or as my friend Annette does, for storing a stellar collection of vintage tablecloths and linens in her dining area. Bookcases like these can also have multiple uses over their lifetime, moving from one room to another as your needs and situation change. Consequently I'm always on the lookout for small and medium sized wooden bookcases. They do turn up, though less often than some of the other pieces in this book. If you find one, buy it—even if you don't know where you might use it at that moment. A bookcase like this can be easily painted and dressed up with moldings to give it more character. Metal shelving too can be rehabilitated; look where used office furniture is sold.

Anything with hooks is also great. Being inherently lazy, I love tossing a coat, scarf, or hat over a hook by the door. Coatracks or other old wall mounted racks with hooks or pegs are extremely useful and practical. If you can't find a wooden one, look for the older and more common utilitarian metal ones that have their own rough charm. Single metal hooks can be cleaned up and mounted on a piece of painted board to hang near a door. And don't forget that there's something deliciously and doubly satisfying about adding pieces to your home that are as practical as they are pretty.

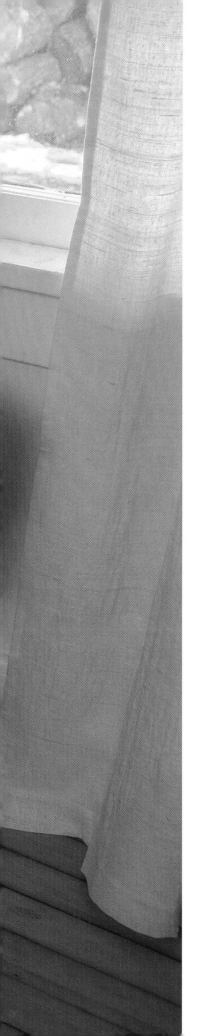

Metal Bar Cart

A lucky find at our local recycling or transfer station, this frame was basically in good shape but missing the shelves. Instead of glass I decided to make new shelves out of some pieces of old distressed wood (which were previously used as table leaves) for a more rustic, industrial look. Replacing the wheels was very easy and the frame was covered with a few coats of spray paint after being cleaned up. Now it is a useful and practical storage piece—ready for service at our next gathering!

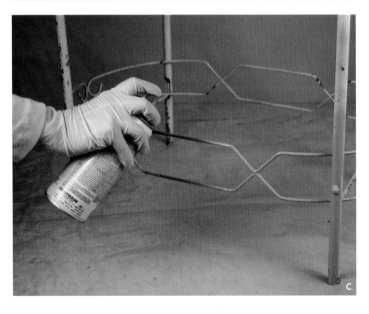

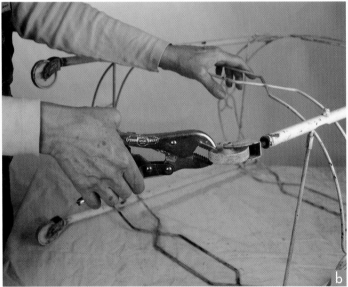

MATERIALS

- Metal cart
- Adjustable pliers
- Paint brush
- Paint remover (like Zip-Strip)
- Fine-grade steel wool or synthetic pad
- Spray paint (here Rust-oleum's Painter's Touch in Nutmeg)
- Protective mask and eyewear
- Rubber gloves
- Hammer
- Rubber wheels

- Manila pattern paper or oaktag
- Pencil
- Scissors
- Marker
- Jig saw
- Scraps of ½- inch thick wood (to fit shelf openings)
- Oil-based wood stain (here Zar in Teak Natural)
- Cheesecloth
- Paint brush
- Polyurethane or tung oil

1 With pliers remove the old wheels from the cart. They should pull out easily. Set aside if they are reusable or discard and replace with new ones as I did here. [photo a and b]

2 Working on one section at a time, apply paint remover to cart following the directions on the container. Work outside or in a well-ventilated space and wear a protective mask, eyewear and rubber gloves. After 15 minutes the paint will start to soften and appear crinkled. Scrape off as much of the softened paint as you can with a putty knife, then use paper towels and fine-grade steel wool or synthetic pad to remove the rest. If necessary, apply a second coat of paint remover and repeat the process. Clean piece with mineral spirits.

3 Spray the cart with 2 or 3 coats of spray paint following the directions on the can, letting them dry between coats.[photo c]

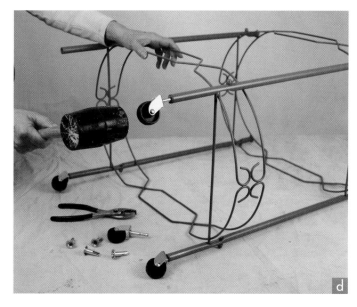

4 Carefully hammer in the new replacement wheels, following directions on the package. (Use a rubber mallet, if you have one, or place a small block of wood in front of a regular hammer if you don't). [Photo d]

5 Make a pattern for the shelves by tracing the opening onto a piece of manila pattern paper or oaktag. Fold the pattern in half both ways to even up the sides with each other and true up the lines if they aren't. Cut out the pattern out using the scissors. Check against the opening again and make any adjustments needed. [Photo e]

6 Lay the pattern on a solid piece of wood, or line up scraps of wood to make the needed width, and trace around the outside edges with the marker. Cut out 2 shelves, an upper and lower, using the jig saw. Sand the outside edges and stain each shelf with wood stain, following the directions on the container. Let dry, and finish with a coat of polyurethane or tung oil. Let dry and insert shelves into cart. [Photo f]

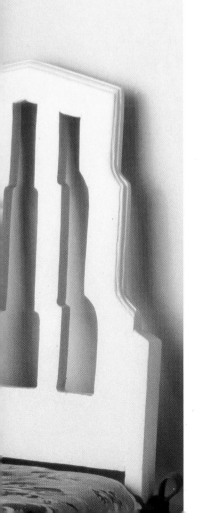

Narrow Bookcase

When I brought this small bookcase home from the Salvation

Army store it was covered in bright orange paint and had 2 layers of adhesive paper on the shelves. I liked its simple shape and aside from the paint it was in very good condition and cost only $35.00. With the addition of some inexpensive stock molding I knew it could be a knockout. Sometimes the price of a plain, but sturdy bookcase is too enticing to pass up, but this doesn't mean you have to settle for its stark lines.

MATERIALS

- Bookcase
- Paint thinner
- Household paintbrush
- Wallpaper scraper
- Power sander
- Corner blocks
- Molding (assorted widths, styles)
- Tape measure
- Soft lead pencil
- Wood saw
- Darker shade satin finish water-based paint
- Lighter shade satin finish water-based paint
- Foam roller / tray
- Primer
- Wood glue
- Masking tape
- Clamps

1 If the shelves are lined with contact paper, remove it by using the paint thinner to loosen the adhesive. Apply the thinner with a brush under the paper and use a wallpaper scraper to remove the loosened paper from the shelves. [photo a]

2 Sand the bookcase as much as necessary to remove the gloss from the existing paint.

3 Cut the different moldings in this sequence: First, lay the corner blocks on the top outside corners, then measure the length of each side below the blocks. Mark the pilaster molding and cut 2 pieces to fit each of the side lengths just measured. Next measure across the width of the bookcase along the front edge of each shelf. Cut out pieces to correspond with each measurement for the front edge of each shelf and the front edges of the top and the bottom shelves. With the pencil, indicate on the back where each piece goes for easy assembly later. [photo b]

4 Paint the inside of the bookcase with 2 coats of the darker paint. Paint the outside of the bookcase with 2 coats of the lighter paint. Prime all the trims, including the molding for the top piece, with the acrylic primer and when the primer is dry, paint with 2 coats of the lighter paint. Let the paint dry thoroughly between coats. [photo c]

5 Lay the bookcase on its back and glue the trims and the molding in place along the sides, shelves, and top and bottom edges with the wood glue. Use masking tape to hold the trim in place as the glue dries if necessary. After the glue is dry, carefully remove the tape and stand the bookcase up. [photo d]

Using Molding

You can find decorative moldings like those I've used here at any lumberyard or, for a better selection, try a specialty building material store. The choices are numerous, from the pilaster moldings and corner blocks used on the long sides to the decorative beaded molding used on the top. Paint the moldings slightly lighter or darker than the bookcase itself for a contrasting accent. You can do this with any type of older bookcase or even with a new one. And if you have two different bookcases that you want to place in the same room, complementary moldings and paint color will give the illusion that they're a matching pair despite slight differences in their respective sizes.

6 To make the frame that sits on top of the bookcase, measure across the sides and front edge of the bookcase top. Cut 3 pieces out of beaded trim to those measurements, mitering the 2 front corners. Glue the pieces together at each corner with the wood glue and then glue the frame to the top of the bookcase, resting it on the front top edge. Clamp until the glue is dry. [photo e]

Metal Storage Bin

Standing bins of this type were originally used in kitchens and pantries to store root vegetables such as onions and potatoes. I love the stamped and pierced metal—it has a modern, almost industrial feel—and it's very functional as well, with its deep bottom shelf, slanted middle shelf for easy access, and the divided storage area on top. By adding a glass top, I made it even more useful without distracting from the clean shape and sleek materials. So while its original function has changed, it still offers the same great storage space in its new setting. The textured glass top (like those found on metal outdoor furniture) adds a pleasing and easy-to-clean surface. Glue rubber bumpers to the underside of the glass to keep it steady and in place on top of the bin.

MATERIALS

- Metal bin
- Wire brush
- Steel wool
- Spray paint (I used Rust-oleum's "Hammered Metal Finish" in silver)
- ¼-inch-thick textured glass
- Wax crayon
- Rubber bumpers
- Clear silicone glue

1 Using a wire brush, remove any loose paint on the bin. Clean any rusty areas with steel wool. Working in a well-ventilated area, spray the bin with 2 coats of paint. Let it dry completely between each coat and after the last coat. [photo a]

2 Measure the top of the bin and add 4 inches to each dimension. Have a piece of ¼-inch-thick glass cut to that size for a top. Make sure to have the edges polished and the corners slightly rounded.

Choosing the Glass Tabletop

Instead of using a piece of plain glass for a tabletop, ask your local glazier to show you samples of the different surface textures and colors they have on hand or can order for you. Some of the available options include rippled, hammered, fluted, cross-hatched, or opaque or tinted glass. As I did here, you can opt for the visual drama that a piece of textured or colored glass will bring to your piece. A thickness of ¼ inch to ½ inch is best for tabletops.

3 Center the glass on the bin, right-side up, and use the crayon to make a mark just to the inside of all 4 corners lightly on the surface of the glass. Turn the glass over and following the corner marks, glue a rubber bumper in each corner just to the inside of each corner mark, using the clear silicone glue. Let it dry completely. [photo b]

4 Turn the glass faceup and place on the bin so the bumpers are positioned just inside of each corner. Remove the crayon marks left on the topside by rubbing lightly with a paper towel.

End Table with Drawer

There's not a lot of detail on this small end table, and it's not particularly well made, so this is exactly the kind of piece that is too easily overlooked at a house sale or flea market. When I bought this table, it wasn't painted white so it was even more unnoticeable. However, I liked the square, vaguely Mission-inspired legs, the recessed shape for the drawer pull, and of course, the affordable price. With a simple piece like this, a coat of paint in an unexpected color like purple transforms it into a much more interesting object. Ultimately, the unusual shade lends the table a distinctive air —a good trick to remember whenever you find this kind of nondescript piece.

MATERIALS

- End table
- Wood glue
- Hammer
- Clamp
- Wood block
- Wood putty
- Putty knife
- Sandpaper
- Household paintbrush
- Satin finish water-based paint

1 Inspect the table and drawer for loose joints. Remove any loose nails and reglue any loose joints in the drawer using wood glue. Apply the glue liberally to the joint and press the 2 sides together. Wipe any excess glue away from the joint with a clean cloth. Renail the joints on the drawer together, if necessary. Clamp or place weights on the joint until the glue sets and is completely dry. [photos a and b]

2 Open the joint on the leg as wide as possible. Apply glue to the legs using the nozzle on the bottle to direct the glue inside the opening. Tap the joints together lightly using a hammer and a wood block to protect the surface. Let the glue dry before proceeding. [photo c]

3 Apply wood putty over any chips, cracks, or other blemishes on the surface. Deeper holes might need more than one application of putty. Push the putty down into the cracks with the putty knife. Draw the knife across the surface, smoothing the excess putty as you go. [photo d]

4 Let the putty dry until it is hard. Sand the surface lightly with fine-grade sandpaper. Prime the piece if necessary. [photo e]

5 Paint with 2 coats of satin finish water based paint. Let dry completely between coats and after the final coat. [photo F]

Loose Drawer Pulls

Many old drawers pull open with wooden knobs that fasten from the inside with a screw. Frequently these screws loosen over time because the threads inside the wooden knob are stripped. To fix, dip a piece of string in wood glue and wind it around the threads of the screw, working it into the grooves. Insert the screw through the drawer and screw the knob back on. Let the glue dry before using.

Distressed Dresser

This three-drawer dresser was found on the streets of NYC, probably taken from an older kitchen that was being renovated. I liked the scale of it and I loved the old copper clam-shell handles. As it was very battered I thought about just stripping and repainint it. But an even better idea occurred—cover parts with some lovely patterned small scraps of wallpaper leftover from a book project at work. There was a lot of clean-up involved as the old layers paint needed to be removed, the piece sanded and the worst nicks filled in with wood putty. Then a new coat of paint was applied to the top edge, and lastly the wallpaper glued on the top and the front.

MATERIALS

- Screwdriver
- Paint remover (like Zip- Strip)
- Household paintbrushes
- Rubber and latex gloves
- Protective mask
- Paint scraper
- Paper towels
- Synthetic steel wool pad
- Mineral spirits
- Spackling paste or wood putty
- Putty knife
- Fine-grade sandpaper or sanding sponge

- Soft lead pencil
- Clear gridded plastic ruler
- Painter's tape
- Semi-gloss finish water-based paint
- Wallpaper of your choice (here Sister Parish Design's Apple in Beige)
- Long metal ruler or straight edge
- Craft knife and cutting mat
- Decoupage medium
- Foam brush
- Power drill

1 With screwdriver remove the handles from the drawers. Set screws aside (or clean if needed with paint remover). [photo a]

2 Working on one section at a time, apply paint remover to dresser, drawers, handles and screws following the directions on the container. Work outside or in a well-ventilated space and wear a protective mask and rubber gloves. After 15 minutes the paint will start to soften and appear crinkled. Scrape off as much of the softened paint as you can with a putty knife, then use paper towels and a synthetic steel wool pad to remove the rest. If necessary, apply a second coat of paint remover and repeat the process. Clean piece with mineral spirits and sand the surfaces lightly. Wipe down.[photo b]

3 Apply a lightweight spackling paste or wood putty over any surface cracks or dents. Deeper holes might need more than one application of the paste. Push the paste down into the cracks with the putty knife. Draw a damp knife across the surface, smoothing the excess paste as you go. Let the putty dry until hard. The paste type of filler does not usually require sanding, but if necessary, sand the surface lightly with fine grade sandpaper.

4 Decide on the width of the border on the dresser top. Here the border is 2½-inches wide. Mark the line lightly with pencil and ruler around the front and side edges. Lay down the painters tape along the outside edge of the line to make a clean edge for the border. If the paint will extend below the top (here the entire top molding is painted) then tape along the lower edge of the molding on the front and sides of the dresser. Paint the border with 2 coats of the paint. Let the paint dry thoroughly between coats and after the last coat. [photo c]

5 When the paint is completely dry, carefully remove the painters's tape. [photo d]

6 Measure and mark the inside border dimensions of the dresser top on the piece of wallpaper. Carefully trim the piece to size using the craft knife, cutting mat and straight edge. Apply decoupage medium to the dresser top and wallpaper using the foam brush and press the paper gently in place. [photo e]

7 Measure and mark the front dimensions of the dresser on the piece of wallpaper. Here I left a strip of wood showing on each side the same as the width of the border. I also covered the whole front in one piece, cutting out the openings for the drawers after the paper was adhered to the surface. Carefully trim the paper to size using the craft knife, cutting mat and straight edge. Apply decoupage medium to the dresser front only using the foam brush and press the paper gently in place. [photo f]

8 When the paper has completely dried, make a long horizontal slit in the center of each drawer opening stopping about 5 to 6 inches from the side edges. Carefully cut angled slits into the 4 corners on each opening and trim

the paper so the outside edges measure about 2 inches wide. Fold the edges over to inside of each drawer opening on all sides and adhere to wood with decoupage medium. [photo g]

9 Coat the entire surface of the dresser including the uncovered wood and the drawer fronts with the decoupage medium using the foam brush. Let it dry completely and apply a second coat. Reattach the drawer handles, drilling new holes if needed.

Odds and Ends

Stuffed under the tables at flea markets or half hidden in thrift shops, old tatty cardboard boxes can yield some of the most interesting candidates for makeovers. That's where the smaller items, like picture frames, can be found, and they have the advantage of being easy to transport, so they can be bought on impulse. Frames can quickly lift a room and I think my walls would feel quite naked without them. Fortunately it's the rare flea market, garage sale, or thrift store that doesn't yield a bumper crop of interesting old frames. I like to keep a cache on hand, from small oval portrait frames to larger rectangular ones and everything in between, to give as gifts—perhaps filled with a print, photo, or even a clipping. Try not to get distracted by the pictures or art in the frames—though sometimes you can find neat images—it's the frames and not what's in them that you're buying. When possible, choose wooden frames rather than plastic and make sure the molding is in good shape. If it is loose, any frame can be reattached at the corners and then repainted or even stripped. The glass can be easily replaced if it is scratched or dull and should never factor into your decision.

Old trays are other frequent finds, and they are extremely useful. Refurbished trays are an ideal way to house even more flea market finds such as a collection of glass bottles, small jewelry boxes, or paperweights. Also, an odd collection of trays repainted in the same color can serve at the dining table as place mats for a more unusual setting. Look for unique shapes and a variety of sizes; a wide range will make them more practical for diverse uses. I also like the way haphazard things take on the appearance of a collection when unified by a tray. There are dozens of possibilities: on a dresser or nightstand to hold reading glasses, water glasses, and other small objects; in the bathroom to organize bottles and makeup; or on a small table to organize a bar area with bottles, decanters, as well as a few glasses.

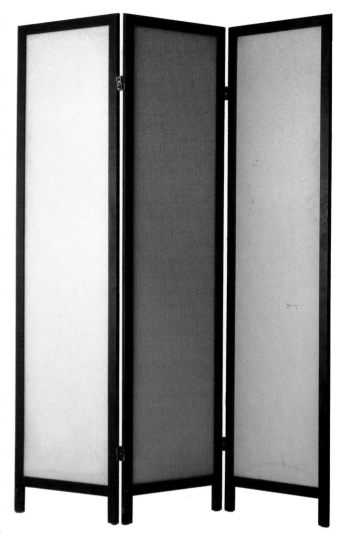

Folding screens represent some of my all time favorite finds because they are both extremely handsome and practical. I like to think of them as instant and flexible architectural devices, whether you're looking to create divisions within one large room or mask some unsightly equipment. For the pack rats among us, screens are especially good for hiding a stash that's gotten out of control. I like to keep one next to my desk to hide the mess that frequently accumulates there. If you cover one side with cork, you've essentially added a large bulletin board adjacent to the desk. Screens can also fit easily in any room and I love the way they can bring instant tranquility to any space by blocking off a distracting area of chaos.

Picture
Frames

Sometimes the best worn treasures come from friends, and these oval framed red rose prints that hail from my friends Charlie and Artemis are prime examples. The frames needed some attention, but the faded floral images had a nostalgic appeal. The prints aren't fancy botanicals, but I find them extremely charming. The red roses brighten against the mat's turquoise line. It's fairly easy to find similar types of floral images already framed or to make your own, as I did here so that the red frames matched the oval framed roses. Just make a photocopy of your chosen flower image on a color copier, adjusting the size to fit your frame. Voilà—instant botanical.

M A T E R I A L S

- Wooden picture frames
- Slip-joint pliers
- Dish soap
- Sandpaper
- Wood glue
- Concentrated artist's acrylic in colors to blend with frame
- Small artist's brush
- Floral image or color copy
- Chipboard

- Picture glass
- Brads
- Double-stick transfer tape (also called ATG or adhesive transfer gum tape)
- Brown kraft paper
- Craft knife and mat
- Metal straightedge ruler
- Small eye hooks
- Lightweight picture wire

1 Remove any picture wire, eye hooks, or paper from the back of the frame. Using the pliers, pull out the small brads holding the inside materials in place. Remove the backing board, the matted picture, and the glass from the frame. Clean any pieces of glass that can be reused and set aside. [photo a]

2 If very grimy, clean the frames with dish soap and a small amount of water, then sand lightly to remove more dirt and grime from the outside edges. If the frame is square and the corners are loose, they can be reglued and nailed as needed. [photo b]

3 Any very worn spots can be touched up with paint by mixing a color to match the frame. Carefully cover the chipped areas on the frame with 2 coats of the paint. Let dry between each coat and after the final coat. [photo c]

Cleaning Old Prints and Glass

To remove grease or grimy spots from an old print, use an art gum eraser or fresh white bread (roll into a ball like a gum eraser) and rub gently over the surface. Work over a piece of paper to catch the crumbs as they fall. Clean old glass with a little ammonia and water. Dry the glass with crumpled balls of newspaper. Remove old masking tape or stickers from glass by applying white vinegar directly to the surface, or use a cloth dampened with vinegar.

4 Reassemble the frame and picture, using the original material, or find a new image to fit the frame. For smaller frames look for art postcards or square-shaped greeting cards at museum stores, which usually have a great selection of botanical and other reproductions. If necessary, use a color copier to resize the image to fit your frame. Otherwise just use the original.

5 To add a new picture, trim off any excess paper so the image will fit the inside of the frame. Cut a new backing board out of the chipboard. To reassemble the frame, first place the cleaned glass in the frame, then the artwork, and last the new chipboard backing. [photo d]

e

f

6 Hold the backing in place by inserting the brads into the frame using the slip-joint pliers, protecting the outside of the frame with a strip of chipboard or cardboard. [photo e]

7 Attach the double-stick transfer tape to the back of the frame. Cut a piece of kraft paper 2 inches larger than the frame. Place the paper on the back of the frame, stretching the paper taut as you secure it to the tape. Trim about ⅛-inch in from the edge, using the craft knife and a straightedge. [photo f]

8 Add the eye hooks a third of the way down the sideof the frame and attach the picture wire to each hook by twisting each side back on itself. Allow some slack in the wire for hanging. [photo g]

Arranging Frames

The three different shapes of frames and the differences in scale play off of one another—each makes the other more interesting. I needed to find a new floral image to fit the square red frame that would complement the other images, but the unusual-looking botanical greeting card I wanted to use was too small for the frame. By making a color enlargement of the card on a copy machine, I was able to use the image I had found. Stacking the frames creates a pleasing arrangement on a narrow hallway wall and the red floral prints tie the different--sized frames together thematically. Hung on the green wall, which is the complementary color of red, the colors in the prints are set off strikingly.

g

Folding Screen

I discovered this folding screen at a neighbor's garage sale for only $10. With the padded fabric panels and beveled mirrored inserts, the screen looks much more expensive. The mirrors also give the screen more

substance, so that it seems more like a piece of furniture, and the added weight gives it some much needed stability, as it was rather light in weight beforehand. Many things can be turned into screens, such as different types of old shutters, sets of multipaned glass doors, and interesting old wood doors or window frames, with or without the glass.

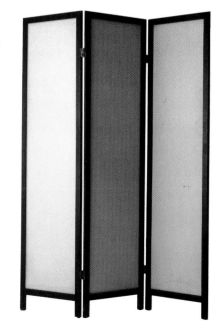

MATERIALS

- Wood-frame folding screen
- Soft lead pencil
- Metal straightedge ruler
- Wood saw
- 1-inch-wide wood lattice
- Clear silicone glue or hot glue gun and glue stick
- Beveled mirrors
- Sandpaper
- Household paintbrush
- Primer
- Satin finish oil-based paint
- Foam-core board
- Scissors
- Cotton fabric
- Polyester batting
- T-pins
- Staple gun and staples
- Double-stick foam mounting tape
- Mirror adhesive
- Utility knife
- Cork sheeting
- Foam roller
- Eggshell finish water-based paint
- Floor adhesive

1 To make the frames for the mirrors, use the pencil to mark a line across each of the panels 12 inches down from and parallel to the top edge. Measure the width of each panel along the marked line and, using a wood saw, cut a strip of lattice to fit across each of the panels. Measure each panel separately, as there might be small differences, and mark each corresponding length of lattice and panel for ease in assembling later. Lay the screen on a flat surface and use the hot glue gun to attach the strips of lattice to each panel following the pencil lines previously marked. The lattice strips should be positioned to fall above the line. Measure each of these framed openings carefully across all 4 sides for width and length, as they might be slightly uneven. Have 3 bevel-edge mirrors cut to fit each of the framed openings.

2 Sand the frame of the screen to degloss the old paint. Apply 1 coat of the primer to the frame, the lattice strips, and the hinges. Apply 2 coats of the oil-based paint to the frame, the lattice, and the hinges. Let it dry thoroughly between coats and after the final coat.

3 To make the fabric-covered padded panels, measure across the width and length of each panel on the screen below the lattice strip. Cut 3 pieces of foam-core board to fit each opening. Mark each corresponding piece of foam-core and panel. Cut a piece of ticking fabric to cover each board, allowing at least 2 inches on each side for wrapping and stretching the fabric around the board. Cut 2 pieces of batting, one the same size as the foam-core board and one 1 inch smaller all around. Center the 2 pieces of batting, with the smaller piece underneath, on the foamcore and center the fabric on top. Insert a t-pin through the fabric and into the edge of the foam-core at the center of one long side. Align the grain of the fabric with the edge of the board, pin the fabric at each corner of the same side, pulling the fabric taut between pins. Wrap the excess fabric to the back of the board, pulling firmly, and staple in place. Complete one side at a time, starting in the center and working out toward the corners. Fold in the excess fabric at the corners and staple in place. [photo a]

4 Lay the screen flat with the lattice side up. Secure the double-stick foam tape to each screen panel close to the edges in each of the openings for the padded fabric panels. Position the padded panels in each screen opening and press into place. Apply the mirror adhesive to the backs of the mirrors and glue the mirrors in place in the framed openings on top of each screen panel. [photo b]

5 To make cork-covered panels on the opposite side of the screen, measure each long panel as directed above. Using the straightedge and a utility knife, cut a length of cork to fit each space. Using the roller, paint the lengths of cork with water-based paint. When dry, glue the cork in place. [photos c, d, and e]

Decorating Tips

Other materials like paper or glass can also be used to decorate your screen. Fabric and paper can be glued onto glass surfaces, and depending on your choice create an opaque or translucent effect—think of Japanese Shoji screens.

Oval Velvet Bench

Old piano benches and other small benches turn up with surprising regularity at thrift stores. The oval-shaped seat and elegant tapered legs give this piano bench a delicate and refined air. Simple white paint and the luxurious sky-blue velvet create a refreshing combination that further enhances the bench's charming details. If the bench you come across is of the more familiar sturdy, rectangular shape, don't despair. These more modern-looking benches usually have less detail and therefore can carry a much bolder fabric, such as a large-scale vintage floral print or a wide awning stripe.

MATERIALS

- Bench
- Screwdriver
- Black permanent marker
- Pliers
- Scissors
- 1-inch-thick foam
- Polyester batting
- Staple gun and staples
- Ruler
- Soft lead pencil
- Upholstery fabric
- Putty knife
- Wood putty
- Sandpaper
- Household paintbrush
- Primer
- Eggshell finish water-based paint

1 Take the bench apart by turning it upside down, locating the screw holes, and unscrewing the top from the base. Set the screws aside. Mark the underside of both the frame and the base with black permanent marker to indicate which way the frame sits in the base. Mark each piece with an X to indicate the sides that go together. After the seat is off, remove the curved backrest if there is one, reserving it for possible use in a future project. [photo a]

2 Remove the screws holding the padded seat to the wooden rim and set the screws aside, carefully marking which screws are used where. Again, mark the corresponding sides on the underside of both seat and frame. [photo b]

3 With the pliers and screwdriver, remove the staples or tacks holding the seat cover in place and remove the old cover. Using the screwdriver, lift up the edge of the staple and pull the loosened staple out with the pliers. Set the old cover aside to use as a pattern. [photo c]

4 Using the wooden oval base as a pattern, cut a piece of foam to fit the base. Cut out new padding from the polyester batting, again using the base as a pattern, allowing 4 inches extra all around for wrapping around the base. Wrap the batting around the base and staple in place, stretching it tightly over the wooden base as you go. Start by stapling the batting to the base with one staple in the middle of each of the opposite long sides, then continue to staple on either side of the centers, alternating from side to side, pulling the batting tight. After continuing to staple the batting to the base for a few more inches on either long side, start stapling the batting to the shorter sides of the oval, starting again in the middle of either opposite end. Ease in the fullness on the curves as you continue around the oval. After you have completed stapling the batting in place, it can be trimmed close to the staples if desired. [photo d]

5 Using the old cover as a pattern, cut a new one out of the upholstery fabric, again adding 4 to 5 inches extra all around. Staple in place over the batting in exactly the same fashion as above and trim the fabric when finished, if desired. [photo e]

6 Using a putty knife, fill the holes in the frame where the curved back piece was attached with wood putty, if necessary. Let dry and sand lightly. Lightly sand the whole frame to help the paint adhere better and smooth out any rough spots.

7 Apply 1 coat of primer to the frame. Sand lightly again and apply 2 coats of water based paint. Let dry thoroughly between coats and after the final coat. [photo F]

8 Place the padded seat in the oval frame and screw in place, using the original screws. Attach the seat to the frame

with the remaining screws, carefully making holes in the fabric if necessary so that the screws connect to the wooden base below.

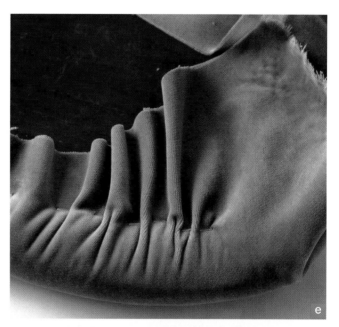

Small Parts

Zip-lock bags or small screw-top jars are great for storing and organizing small parts like screws that you need to use later. Label the outside of the bag or container so there is no confusion when you are putting things back together.

La Poste Pillow

I've been noticing a trend for decorative throw pillows with lettering or writing on them in the stores and recent issues of the decorating magazines. Using this vintage mailbag from France, that I had acquired sometime in the past, I created my own interpretation of this popular idea. The addition of some scraps of satin ribbon adds a bit of sheen and a subtle hint of color to the pillow. I used the ribbons only on one side and left the other plain for an alternate look.

1 Wash the sack if necessary and carefully press on both sides using the iron and plenty of steam. With clear plastic gridded ruler and pencil, mark a rectangle (here 16 x 22 inches) or square the size of your pillow, adding ½-inch all around for seam allowance. Pay attention to where the lettering falls on each piece and look to avoid any worn out areas. Mark 2 pieces, one for the front and one for the back. [Photo a]

2 Carefully cut out the front and back with the fabric scissors. [Photo b]

3 Measure and cut lengths of ribbons to fit between the rows of lettering on the front side only, or to your taste. Pin the ribbons in place. Here I used 5 lengths of ribbons, with 2 ribbons layered together and stitched before sewing them to the pillow front. With the sewing machine, straight stitch down one side and then other, working in the same direction on each ribbon. [Photo c]

4 With the right sides facing, pin the front and back together along the side seams and along the bottom edge, leaving a 7-inch opening on one bottom edge. Machine stitch them together, allowing for the ½-inch seam allowance. [Photo d]

5 Press the seams open and trim off any extra material on the inside corners. Turn the pillow cover to the right side, stuff with insert. Pin the opening closed and stitch closed by hand using an overcast stitch. [Photo e]

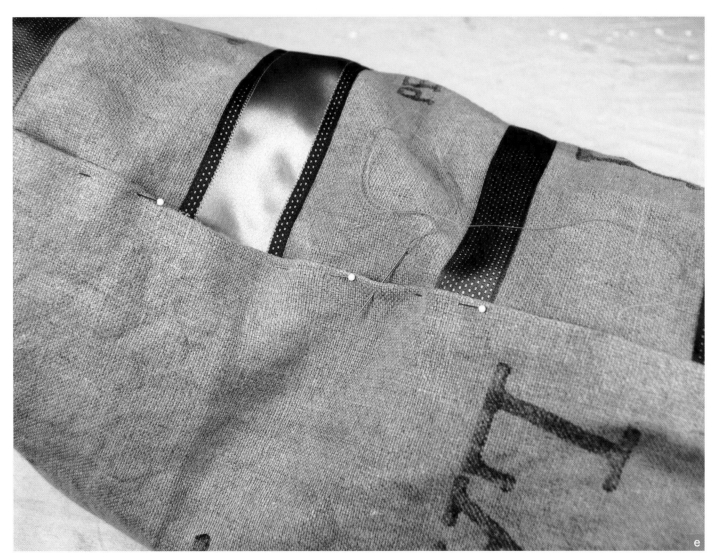

Carved Mirrored Panel

My father gave me this old carved wood panel, it originally came from an upright piano and formed the front section where the sheet music rested. Sometime later, I noticed a photo in a magazine of a mirrored and carved panel hanging over a bed, serving as the headboard. I immediately thought about the piano panel. And even though the panel now looks very different from my original inspiration, in the end, it suits my needs and the style of this bedroom perfectly.

a

b

MATERIALS

- Wood panel
- Sandpaper
- Acrylic primer
- Pale color satin finish water-based paint
- White water-based paint
- Large household paintbrush
- Cheesecloth
- Beveled-edge mirror
- Mirror adhesive
- Awl
- Hangers/screws
- Heavy-duty picture wire
- Rubber bumpers

1 Sand the panel lightly and prime the whole piece, including the moldings, with the primer. Paint with 2 coats of the pale satin finish water-based paint, letting it dry between coats. Let dry completely. To bring out the details of the carving, make a wash by diluting 1 part white water-based paint with 8 parts water. With the large paintbrush, lightly and quickly brush out the wash, letting it puddle a little in the carved-out areas. [photo a]

2 Using a pad of cheesecloth, dab at the wash to soften it. Then wipe off most of the wash from the highlights of the moldings and the flat surfaces of the panel, leaving some remaining in the recesses. Let dry completely. [photo b]

3 Measure the center panel opening and have a beveled-edge mirror cut to fit. Glue the mirror into the opening with mirror adhesive following the manufacturer's directions. [photo c]

4 Using an awl, mark the placement for the hangers about one third down from the upper edge on each side. Screw the hangers onto the back of the panel. Thread heavy-duty picture wire 3 or 4 times through one hanger, twisting the end back on itself. Stretch the wire across the back to the opposite side and thread through the second hanger as before, allowing enough slack so the wire

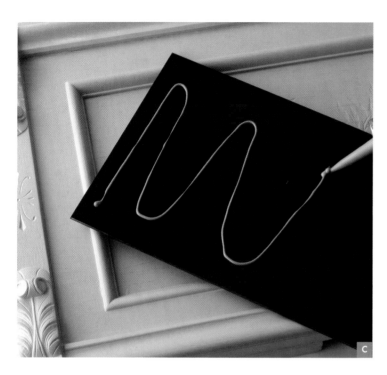

falls about 2 to 3 inches from the top of the panel when hung. Secure rubber bumpers to the back lower corners of the panel.

5 Hang the panel from two heavy-duty screws firmly anchored into the studs behind the wall. Two separate hangers spaced on either side of the center point will work to distribute the weight evenly, so the panel will hang straighter and more securely. Think carefully about the correct height when you hang the panel. The lower edge should be positioned just high enough so that your head will not bump into it when you are sitting up in bed. You could also attach it directly to the bed frame by screwing 2 x 4's (painted to match) onto the back of the panel and attaching them to the bed frame.

Replacing and Moving the Molding

If the piece is missing any molding, it can be replaced, or perhaps resituated from another section. Measure the space and cut a piece of the matching molding to replace the missing section. Alternatively, remove a piece of unneeded molding and reposition it, as I did here in the center section. I also needed to add new molding to the lower edge of the right outside panel, where it was missing. Because the size of the new molding was slightly different than the original I decided to replace the piece of original molding on the left with new molding so that both of the outside lower edges would match. Add a piece of wood underneath if necessary to provide a surface for the extra molding to sit on. Glue in place first before attaching the molding. Glue the new piece of molding and any recycled piece of molding in place with the wood glue. Clamp or place weights on the molding until the glue sets and is completely dry. [photo d]

Tubular Metal Stool

A simple tubular metal stool with an interesting shaped wire pattern caught my eye at a flea market. I had a large black leather bag leftover from another project. I had purchased it at the Salvation Army to use the straps for another item—and put it away for future use as the black leather in the bag was of good quality. It yielded just enough to cover this small seat and that, with the addition of white paint, makes the stool into a very graphic object.

MATERIALS

- Wire Stool
- Pliers or wrench
- Screwdriver
- Protective mask and eyewear
- Rubber gloves
- Household paintbrush
- Paint remover (like Zip-Strip)
- Fine-grade steel wool or synthetic pad
- Mineral spirits
- Spray paint (here Rust-oleum Protective Enamel in White)
- Permanent marker
- Scissors
- Polyester batting
- Black leather scrap
- Staple gun and staples

1 With a pliers or wrench remove the nuts and bolts holding the seat to the chair Use Liquid Wrench if the nuts are frozen. Set the seat aside until later. [Photo a]

2 Working on one section at a time, apply paint remover to the stool following the directions on the container. Work outside or in a well-ventilated space and wear a protective mask, eyewear and rubber gloves. After 15 minutes the paint will start to soften and appear crinkled. [Photo b]

3 Scrape off as much of the softened paint as you can with a putty knife, then use paper towels and fine-grade steel wool or synthetic pad to remove the rest. If necessary, apply a second coat of paint remover and repeat the process. Clean piece with mineral spirits.[photo c]

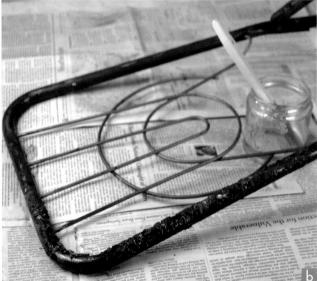

4 Spray the stool with 2 or 3 coats of white spray paint following the directions on the can, letting them dry between coats. Set aside.

5 With the pliers and screwdriver, remove the staples or tacks holding the seat cover in place and remove the old cover. Using the screwdriver, lift up the center of each staple and twist so one end is loose. Pull the loosened staples out with the pliers. Discard the old seat cover and padding, retaining the wood base.[photo d]

6 Using the wood base as a pattern, trace an outline on the polyester batting with the permanent marker. Trim the batting to fit the base using a scissors. Make a new cover for the seat by tracing around the base on the leather, adding 4 to 5 inches extra all around. Trim the leather with the scissors.[photo e]

7 Reinsert the set aside bolts used to attach the seat to the stool into the holes in the wood base. Place the base on the batting and new cover. Wrap the leather cover around the base and staple it in place, stretching it firmly over the base as you go. Start stapling in the middle of two opposite sides, and then do the same on the other two opposite sides and then add a staple in between those. Continue to staple around the circle spacing staples about ½-inch apart, pulling the cover tight, and easing the leather folds in as you go. [Photo f]

Tools

I strongly recommend investing in the three items below before starting on any of the projects in this book. Though you can do any of the projects in the book without them, they will save you hours of prep time and more than repay your investment in the long term.

- Although you can easily sand small pieces by hand, having a lightweight orbital sander will make short work of most sanding chores, especially if you are planning to do two or more furniture makeovers. Look for one that's light and easy for you to maneuver. It will save you hours of preparation time.

- I also suggest buying a cordless electric drill, which is both a power drill and a screwdriver. I found it very liberating when I finally decided to invest in one. In addition to using it for your makeovers, I guarantee that you will find almost daily use for it around the house. Look for one that's on the small side; it will be easier to handle, as the battery pack can make them awkward and heavy. Hold a few in your hand to judge which one feels the most comfortable.

- It's also a sound investment to acquire a few good-quality paintbrushes that won't lose their bristles. If you take proper care of them, you will have them forever, and you will be thankful every time you paint not to be picking out loose bristles left behind by cheap paintbrushes.

ESSENTIAL TOOL KIT

- adjustable wrench
- cordless electric drill
- craft knife
- hammer
- masking tape
- metal-edge ruler
- orbital sander
- pencil
- permanent marker

- pliers
- putty knife
- retractable metal tape measure
- rubber mallet
- screwdrivers, both flat-head and Phillips
- single-edge razor blades
- staple gun and staples
- wire cutters
- wood glue

ESSENTIAL SEWING KIT

- clear plastic gridded ruler
- cloth tape measure
- hand-sewing needles
- iron glass-head straight pins
- pencil
- pincushion
- rotary cutter and mat
- seam ripper or single-edge razor blades
- scissors for fabric
- scissors for paper
- spray bottle (use for water when ironing)
- thread in white, black, and beige
- water-soluble fabric marker

ESSENTIAL PAINTING KIT

- combing tool
- cheesecloth
- large and small household paintbrushes
- painter's tape
- paper towels
- soft cotton rags (old white cotton T-shirts and make the best rags)
- square- and round-tip artist's brushes

ESSENTIAL REFINISHING KIT

- 6-in-1 painter's tool
- fine-grade sandpaper or sanding sponge
- fine-grade steel wool
- heavy-duty rubber gloves
- old toothbrushes and dental pick
- plastic scraper
- plastic stripping brush
- protective mask and eye wear
- wire brush

ESSENTIAL CRAFT KIT

- cotton swabs
- craft glue
- craft knife and cutting mat
- decoupage medium
- disposable foam brushes
- glaze medium
- latex gloves
- masking and white tape
- nail scissors
- repositional spray adhesive
- small bottles of artist's pigment in basic colors (white, black, red, yellow, blue, green, violet, orange, raw umber, burnt sienna)
- small spray bottles
- stencil brush
- square-and round-tip artist's brushes
- scissors

Cleaning

HOW TO CLEAN WOOD

• Fill a container with warm water and add a small amount of a mild dishwashing detergent (like Ivory). Dip a soft, clean rag in the water, wring out well, and wipe the wood with the damp rag.

• Do not soak the wood or let the water sit on it. Wipe it dry with clean rags or paper towels.

HOW TO CLEAN WICKER

• Fill a container with warm water and add a cleaning agent (like Soilex) or, if it's just surface dirt, a small amount of a mild dishwashing detergent (like Ivory). Dip a soft, clean sponge in the water and wipe the wicker with the damp sponge.

• Use an old toothbrush to clean in the corners and crevices that are hard to reach with the sponge.

• Rinse well and let the wicker dry outdoors in the sun.

• Rub a small amount of linseed oil into the surface of natural unpainted wicker to restore its luster.

HOW TO REMOVE LIGHT RUST ON IRON OR STEEL

• Apply naval jelly to the surface. Leave on for 5 to 20 minutes. Rinse off with water. Repeat if any rust remains. You can also rub the surface lightly with a fine-grade steel wool pad over the naval jelly.

• Alternatively, for very light rust, rub the surface with a steel wool pad dipped in vegetable oil.

• Use these techniques only on steel or iron. Do not use on aluminum or chrome.

HOW TO REMOVE LIGHT STAINS ON CHROME-PLATED TUBULAR STEEL AND ALUMINUM

• Use a rubbing compound formulated for chrome / aluminum.

• Apply a light coat of silicone furniture polish to protect the finish.

HOW TO REMOVE LIGHT STAINS ON MARBLE

• Rub light stains with toothpaste and a clean rag using lots of elbow grease.

• Wipe clean with a damp rag or paper towel. Dry with a clean rag or paper towel.

HOW TO POLISH SMALL METAL FITTINGS

• Use a small amount of toothpaste and an old toothbrush to give a quick polish to small metal fittings like knobs and hinges.

• Wipe clean with a damp rag or rinse in water and dry.

HOW TO REMOVE RUST STAINS ON FABRIC

• Dip half a lemon in salt. Rub it directly on the stain and let it sit for a few minutes.

• Stretch the fabric over the top of any heat-resistant (metal or tempered-glass) bowl,

• Pour boiling water through the fabric until the stain is out.

HOW TO REMOVE OLD TAPE OR STICKERS ON GLASS

• Rub the surface of the sticker or tape with a cloth dampened with white vinegar.

• Or rub a small amount of peanut butter into the sticker until it dislodges.

• Rinse with soapy water.

• Nail polish remover, turpentine, and prewash spray can also be effective in loosening the glue on stickers.

HOW TO CLEAN GLASS OR GLASSWARE

• Fill a spray bottle with water to which you have added a small amount of ammonia and spray the solution on the surface of the glass.

• Dry and polish the glass with wadded-up newspapers.

• Wash glassware in warm, soapy water, adding a small amount of white vinegar to the rinse water.

• If glassware remains cloudy, try soaking it overnight in a bowl of water to which you have added a denture-cleaning tablet.

Repairing

HOW TO TIGHTEN JOINTS ON WOODEN FURNITURE

• Use a shim to tighten rectangular joints. This works especially well for the stretchers that fit in the legs of chairs and tables, which frequently become loose through hard use.

• Make a shim out of a small scrap of hardwood. It can be of even thickness or slightly tapered, but it should be as wide as the hole.

• Apply glue to the hole and drive the shim into place. Apply more glue and reassemble the joint. Wipe any excess glue off with a damp rag.

• Use cloth strips for round or square joints. Cut cloth (from an old sheet or shirt) into strips. The strips should be narrower than the end of the part you're inserting.

• Place the strips over the end of the part in the form of an X. Trim the strips on the sides so they are about two thirds of the depth of the joint–the cloth will stretch when the pieces are joined.

• Apply glue to the hole and reassemble the joint. Trim any cloth protruding after the joint is assembled with a razor blade and wipe any excess glue off with a damp rag.

HOW TO FILL SMALL CRACKS, SURFACE DENTS, HOLES, AND OTHER SURFACE BLEMISHES ON WOODEN FURNITURE

• Working on a clean surface, use a putty knife to apply a lightweight spackling paste (like UGL 222) or wood putty over any cracks or other dents. Deeper holes might need more than one application of the paste.

• Push the paste down into the cracks with the putty knife. Draw a damp knife across the surface, smoothing the excess paste as you go. Let the putty dry until it is hard.

• The paste type of filler does not usually require sanding, but if necessary, sand the surface lightly with fine-grade sandpaper.

HOW TO WIRE A NEW LAMP OR REWIRE AN OLD LAMP

• Use a new lamp socket, if needed, or the original one if it is in good shape. With a prewired cord set (where the plug is already attached to the lamp cord) you will be done in a flash.

- For a regular lamp socket, insert the cord set through opening in socket cap, pull out some extra wire at the top so you have plenty to work with. Split the wire and make an underwriter's knot within the cap.

- Strip ends of each wire if needed and twist the strands of each wire tightly together. Wrap the neutral wire (covered with ridged insulation) around the silver terminal screw on the socket interior in a clockwise manner, tightening the screw securely over the loop. Wrap the smoother hot wire around the brass terminal on the socket interior in a clockwise manner and tighten. Make sure all the conductors on under the screw head.

- Place the socket shell with insulating cardboard sleeve over the lamp socket, and snap the shell on the socket cap, making sure it is locked in place.

Getting Started

Careful surface preparation will give you the best results. Frequently you can paint over the original finish if you take the time to prepare the surface.

HOW TO PREPARE WOODEN PIECES FOR PAINTING OR REFINISHING

- Use a power sander or sandpaper to sand any previously painted surface to provide a smooth, nonglossy, paintable surface (be sure to wear a protective mask).

- If the finish or paint is too thick, badly cracked, sticky, or uneven, it can be removed with paint remover, following the directions on the container. If you decide to remove the old paint or finish entirely, sand the piece when you are done.

- Remove sanding dust with a soft rag before proceeding to paint or refinish.

HOW TO PREPARE METAL PIECES FOR PAINTING OR RESURFACING

- Use a wire brush or sander remove any loose, flaking metal or paint to provide a smooth, paintable surface.

- If there are too many layers of paint to sand, they can be removed with a paint remover especially formulated for metal, following the directions on the container.

- If the piece is very rusty, apply a product like Rust-oleum Rust Reformer, which bonds with the metal to form a smooth, paintable surface.

Refinishing

HOW TO REMOVE OLD PAINT OR MULTIPLE FINISHES FROM WOOD, METAL, OR WICKER FURNITURE

- Use a paint remover specifically formulated for your surface. There are removers for use on either metal or wood surfaces. Work outside where possible or in a well-ventilated work space.

- Wear heavy-duty rubber gloves, protective eyewear and mask. Apply the remover liberally with an old paintbrush. Let the remover stand for 15 to 20 minutes until the finish is softened and the surface appears crinkly. Don't let the remover dry out.

- Remove the loosened paint or finish by scraping it with a plastic scraper, 6-in-1 painter's tool, rounded-edge putty knife, a plastic stripping brush or steel wool or synthetic steel wool pads, or a combination of the above. Which tool you use depends on the type of surface involved.

- For wicker, keep the surface wet by applying the remover with a spray bottle. Use a plastic stripping brush to remove the finish. Use a toothbrush (or cut down an old paintbrush) dipped in mineral spirits or the solvent recommended on the paint remover container to finish cleaning the surface.

- Wipe off as much of the remaining finish as possible using crumpled paper towels. Dip a pad of fine-grade steel wool in the solvent recommended (generally mineral spirits) on the container and scrub the surface for a final cleaning. Wipe the surface dry with a clean rag.

HOW TO REMOVE HEAVY RUST ON IRON OR STEEL FURNITURE

- Remove heavy rust by using a circular power drill with a wire brush attachment. Grind as much of the loose rust and corrosion off the surface as you can.

- Use a wire brush to clean in the corners and crevices that are hard to reach with the drill. Wear heavy-duty gloves, a protective mask and eyewear.

HOW TO ACHIEVE A BRUSHED FINISH ON STRIPPED STEEL FURNITURE

• For an attractive brushed-metal finish, attach a medium wire brush to a power drill and work slowly and evenly across the surface to smooth and polish it.

• Keep the drill moving to achieve an overall brushed-satin finish.

• The surface will need to be protected, so finish it with a coat or two of clear satin spray lacquer.

HOW TO MAINTAIN A RUSTED SURFACE ON METAL

• To maintain the look of rusted metal, first brush the surface with a wire brush to remove loose particles, then rub the piece with boiled linseed oil and let it soak in overnight.

• Wipe off the excess linseed oil and protect the surface with a final spray of clear matte acrylic sealer from a craft store.

Painting, Staining and Varnishing

HOW TO PREPARE WOOD FOR PAINTING

• Sand the piece with a power sander or by hand with sandpaper or a sanding sponge.

• Remove the dust with a tack rag or a brush or wipe the surface down with a damp paper towel. Let it dry thoroughly.

HOW TO PRIME WOOD BEFORE PAINTING

• If you need to prime the surface, I recommend using an primer like Benjamin Moore's Fresh Start, which adheres well to a variety of surfaces, is quick drying, and cleans up with water.

• Apply one coat and let it dry thoroughly. Sand the surface lightly and remove the dust before proceeding.

HOW TO PRIME METAL BEFORE PAINTING

• Metal can be primed, as above for wood, with an acrylic primer.

• If the piece is very rusty, treat it first with Rust-Oleum Rust Reformer, a product that chemically converts rust into a smooth, paintable surface. There's no need to sand all the way down to the bare metal; just remove as much of the rust as possible. Apply the Rust Reformer as directed on the package.

• For further protection, follow this by priming with a rust-preventive metal-specific primer.

HOW TO PAINT WITH WATER-BASED PAINT

• For outdoor pieces, look for either a satin-finish paint like Benjamin Moore's MoorGlo or MoorGard (which have a slight sheen) or an enamel finish like Benjamin Moore's Impervex (which has a high-gloss finish).

• For indoor pieces, use any paint formulated for indoor use like Benjamin Moore's Regal AquaPearl (which has a slight sheen) or Benjamin Moore's Regal AquaGlo (which has semi-gloss finish).

• Two coats of paint are best, but sometimes one will do. Let the first coat dry, then sand the surface lightly and remove the dust before applying the second coat. Let pieces dry thoroughly before using them.

HOW TO AGE NEW PAINT

• New paint can be given a vintage look by applying a transparent glaze to the surface after the paint has dried. Add a small amount of raw umber to some water or glaze medium and lightly brush the mixture onto the painted item.

- If it still looks too new once the glaze dries, repeat the procedure or try lightly washing the piece with water.

HOW TO STAIN UNFINISHED OR STRIPPED WOOD SURFACES

- Make a pad of clean cheesecloth, apply the stain over the surface, working on a small area at a time. Allow the stain to penetrate the surface no longer than three to five minutes.
- While the stain is still wet, use a clean section of cheesecloth to wipe off the excess, working in the direction of the wood grain. Let dry and repeat again if desired.

HOW TO VARNISH STRIPPED AND UNPAINTED WOOD SURFACES

- Use a protective, penetrating oil finish (like Formby's Tung Oil Finish in low gloss) for a natural, classic look. This type of finish penetrates the wood and dries clear, allowing the natural beauty of the wood to shine.
- After preparing the surface, rub a small amount of tung oil into the wood using a soft, clean rag. Allow it to dry and buff it with a fine-grade steel wool pad. Wipe it down with a clean rag and repeat until you have achieved the desired finish, then let it dry completely.

Setting up Your Work Space

THINGS TO HAVE ON HAND BEFORE STARTING

- Paper towels
- Clean rags
- Ziploc bags in assorted sizes
- Large plastic trash bags (I hang one up nearby)
- Rubber gloves
- Plastic goggles
- Protective mask and/or respirator
- Appropriate solvent for paint or refinisher
- Assorted containers and buckets (save your larger metal food cans; they make good containers for solvents, paint, mixing, etc.)

GETTING READY TO REFINISH

- It's best to work outdoors, as stripping is messy and smelly. If that is not possible, a basement or garage, with proper ventilation, is another choice.

- Spread a heavy-duty drop cloth on the floor or work surface and layer with newspapers or a plastic drop cloth.
- Use a fan to increase ventilation, and open all doors and windows.
- Wear heavy-duty rubber gloves, safety glasses, and a respirator or a protective mask.
- Have paper towels handy.

GETTING READY TO PAINT

- Painting is messy and sloppy, so work a safe distance from walls and furniture.
- Spread a heavy-duty drop cloth on the floor or work surface, or layer the work area with newspapers.
- Open doors and windows if you are working inside.
- If you are working outside, be sure to paint only when it is not windy or very humid.
- Have a bucket of water or solvent handy for brush cleanup.
- If you have to stop before you are finished, place the brush (or roller) in a plastic bread bag or other thin plastic bag, squeeze out the air, and tie it firmly closed around the handle.
- If you can't resume painting in a few hours, place the whole wrapped brush (or roller) in a large Ziploc bag and pop it in the freezer. It will stay wet indefinitely.

GETTING READY TO SPRAY PAINT

- Outdoors is best, but spray painting can be done indoors in a very well ventilated area.
- Open all the windows and doors and wear a respirator or protective mask.
- Prepare a large work area, as for painting. For smaller objects, you can construct a mini spray booth by cutting the top and one side off a smallish cardboard box.
- The best way to ensure even coverage is to spray many light coats. Move the can in a slow, even movement across the object being sprayed. Don't stop when you get to the edge but continue slightly over the sides and then go back in the other direction. Continue until the object is evenly coated with paint.

Resources

LIGHTING AND LAMP MAKING SUPPLIES

Grand Brass Lamp Parts
212-226-2567 Fax 212 226 2573
www.grandbrass.com
A very large section of new and replacement lamp and lighting parts

Just Shades
21 Spring St. New York, NY 10012
212-966-2757 fax 212-334-6129
www.justshadesny.com
A wide selection of ready-made paper, linen and fabric lamp shades, they also make custom shades. If you go in person, be sure to bring your lamp.

The Lamp Shop
PO Box 3606 Concord, NH 03302-3606
603-244-1603 fax 603-224-6677
www.lampshop.com
Lamp-shade crafting supplies, materials, and other small shade-related lamp parts. They also carry a useful series of instructional booklets for making different types of lamp shades.

FABRICS, UPHOLSTERY, TRIMS, WALLPAPER AND SEWING SUPPLIES

Calico Corners
800-213-6366
www.calicocorners.com
Discount top–quality home furnishing fabrics and decorating services Check website for store locations

Clotilde
PO Box 7500 Big Sandy, TX 75755
800-545-4002
www.clotilde.com
Catalog and online retailer of sewing notions and supplies

Joann Fabric and Craft
888-739-4120
www.joann.com
Fabrics, trims, upholstery and sewing supplies
Check website for store locations

Just Scandinavian
161 Hudson Street New York, NY 10013
212-334-2556 Fax 212-334-2557
www.justscandinavian.com
Home furnishing retail store, online retailer for Josef Frank fabrics

Martin Albert Interiors
9 E 19th St New York, NY 10003
212-673-8000 Fax 212-673-8006
www.martinalbert.com
Custom furniture & window treatments

Mokuba
55 W 38th Street New York, NY 10018
212-869-8900 Fax 212-869-8970
www.mokubany.com
Outstanding ribbons, passementerie and lace trims
Call for retailer information

Oilcloth International
134 N. Avenue 61, Building #101
Los Angeles, Ca 90042
323-344-3967 Fax 323 259-5951
www.oilcloth.com
Patterned oilcloth
Call or email for retailer information

Rose Brand
4 Emerson Lane Secaucus, NJ 07094
800-223-1624
201-809-1730 Fax 201-809-1851

www.rosebrand.com
Canvas, muslin and outdoor fabrics
Catalog and online retailer

Sister Parish Design
914-234-7452
www.sisterparishdesign.com
Homefurnishing fabrics and wallpaper
Call or email for information

CRAFT, PAINT, AND OTHER SUPPLIES

A.C. Moore
130 A.C. Moore Drive Berlin, New Jersey 08009.
Retail craft and art supplies
www.acmoore.com
Check website for store locations

Benjamin Moore
51 Chestnut Ridge Road Montvale, NJ 07645
800-344 0400
www.benjaminmoore.com
Manufacturer of exterior and interior paint
Call or email for retailer information

Blick Art Materials
P.O Box 1267 Galesburg, Il 61402
800-723-2787 Fax 800-621-8293
www.dickblick.com
Catalog and online retailer for art, craft
and mosaic supplies

Michael's Arts & Crafts
800-642-4235
www.michaels.com
Retail craft and art supplies.
Check website for store locations

HARDWARE, LUMBER AND TOOLS

Dykes Lumber Company
1899 Park Avenue Weehawken, NJ 07087
201-867-0391 Fax 201-867-1674
www.dykeslumber.com
Check website for store locations, catalog and online retailer
for specialty moldings

Home Depot
800-353-3199
www.homedepot.com
Check website for store locations, online retailer

Lowe's
800-445-6937
www.lowes.com
Check website for store locations, online retailer